3/6/15

To my beautiful Noshin,

I love You and am
so blessed to have
you in my life !

♡ always,

Love & Blessings

S.O.S Sink or Swim

HANNAH BONDE

authorHOUSE®

AuthorHouse™
1663 Liberty Drive
Bloomington, IN 47403
www.authorhouse.com
Phone: 1 (800) 839-8640

Published by AuthorHouse 02/04/2015

ISBN: 978-1-4969-6883-8 (sc)
ISBN: 978-1-4969-6882-1 (hc)
ISBN: 978-1-4969-6881-4 (e)

Library of Congress Control Number: 2015901865

Hannah Bonde was born in Gothenburg, Sweden in 1970. Her father, a Finnish native and with a Swedish mother, she became a woman of character and Hannah learned the true meaning of survival and sacrifice. At the age of fifteen she met the one she believed would be the love of her life. Fifteen years later the once love of her life had become someone to be feared rather than loved. After enduring constant verbal and physical abuse Hannah managed to escape from the grasp of her soon would be husband. In 1999, she found herself at Los Angeles International Airport with almost no money, no home and no family or friends. Absent creature comforts and plan for her future, she kept moving forward with the hope of a better life just over the horizon. Hannah managed to start from scratch, build a new life for herself, working for the rich and famous. Her passion for helping other abused women compelled Hannah to share her story in hopes that it will give other women the courage to free themselves from their own private hell as she did hers.

A few words from my heart……..

First I want to thank God for always watching over and protecting me. Without true faith and beliefs, I would've been dead long time ago.

Even though I was not brought up in a church, I have always believed in 'something', always been praying and that is what kept me going, made me a survivor and to never give up. Starting over in a new country, there were times I didn't know how to make it but I told myself "I don't know how I'm going to do it, but I will….. somehow" and I always did, somehow.

To my mother and father, R.I.P! I miss you all day every day but I know both of you finally have peace up in the Kingdom and I have some amazing guardian angels.

To my sisters, I love you so much and I wouldn't be where I am today if it wasn't for your love, support and prayers along the years.

To my loving Pit bull pup Honey B, the apple of my eye, who lives to love and protect me, you are my little princess and you are priceless. Best thing I've ever had in my life. Dogs, all breeds, truly are a reflection of their owners!

Last but not least, to everyone else in my life, you all are amazing and I'm blessed to have you all in my life.

Love & Gratitude always
Hannah,
www.habonde.com
FB; Damned if I Do, Dead if I Don't

The Wedding March starts, the church doors swing open and I start walking slowly down the aisle towards the tall man, the man who, in a few minutes will be my husband. He is looking towards me, but I can't quite see his face. As I look at all the people gathered to join with us in celebrating our wedding day, I feel like Cinderella as I walk down the aisle in my long, white sleeveless wedding dress and my golden shoes. All the guests and lookers-on are turned and looking at me. I couldn't be happier. I am now only an arm's length away, the tall man reaches for me, and expecting a gentle reach for my arm, I am grabbed hard by my hand, as he pulls me close to him saying,

"I told you, you can run but you can't hide."

Now I see his face and I panic. It's Jared! As I struggle to twist myself free from his grasp on my wrist, my heart is pounding hard. Boom! Boom! I turn around and I see that the church is now a cemetery and the guests are corpses, laughing and pointing at me. I hear his voice like an echo, *mine forever, mine forever.*

'No-oo-oo-o,'

I am awakened by my own screams and realize that I'm alone in bed. I'm sweaty and my heart is beating out of my chest. Then I remember that I am actually in California, in a hotel room, and safe. I get out of bed and go to the bathroom, splash water on my face to wake myself up and also to erase the nightmare as I said to myself,
'You'll be ok Hannah. You just need to let the past go.'

November 5th 1999

I looked at the clock it was only 6.30 a.m. After a night's questionable rest, I was still so tired and tense. And I was afraid. It felt like I had a buzz but when I tried to go back to sleep, I couldn't. I stayed in bed for another hour or so before I got up and called my dad to tell him I had arrived safely and to give him the phone number where he could reach me.

"Hannah, I'm in a rush and on my way to the airport myself. Let me call you back, when I arrive to Switzerland, okay?"
I should have known better and be used to this by now. Because every time my father brushed me off like this, it hurts. Hurts just as it did when I was a little girl and he didn't have time to listen to me.

I pulled a chair over to the window and looked out. The view wasn't the most beautiful but you could see the airplanes coming and going. They were so close it was amazing. I had never seen planes so close from anywhere in Sweden. Apparently, I fell asleep sitting there, because the next time I looked at the clock, it was 2.30 p.m.
'Hannah, you better get started if you're going to get something done today.' I pulled out the Yellow Pages and realized that there was a book for each area so the areas must be big here. I needed to get cheaper lodgings, at least cheaper than this hotel, and that by tomorrow. I only had $250 to my name.

I called one place listed in an ad with rooms for rent, but there was nothing available. I started to feel stressed again. All these random thoughts went through my mind. *'What did I do and what had I gotten myself into, and how was it going to end? How easy would it be to find a place?'* I had little money, nowhere to go and in a country where I didn't know anybody.' *I must be crazy!'* Those thoughts kept repeating in my mind. But I know and I am sure that if I would've stayed, I'd be dead by now!

At this point in time, there is no idea to ask my parents for help. My mom would say she doesn't have any money, and my dad would just tell me to go back to Sweden and that is not going to happen. I didn't leave the room the whole day, not even to eat because I had to save and carefully plan how to spend the few dollars I had left. I made myself a cup of coffee in the room. While I was getting dressed I started to feel claustrophobic. I needed to get out of here, if just for a little. I was too restless to think clearly.

At 9:00 p.m. I left the room and took the elevator down to the lobby where I ran into Benson, the nice man who drove the shuttle yesterday. I asked him if he knew of any place where there were rooms for rent and not too expensive.

"No I don't, off the top of my head, but I will keep my eyes open for you."

"Thank you, I appreciate it, but I need something real soon."
We said goodbye and while I started to walk out the front doors, Benson said

"Lady be careful, this is not a very good area, and it is not so safe out there."

"Thank you Benson", I said but what really crossed my mind at that moment was *'Well at least it's safer here than Sweden for me.'* I was starving at this point and walked into McDonalds, which was right outside the hotel. I ordered a hamburger and after getting my food I sat down at a table close to the wall. While I ate, I looked around at the people around me. A couple holding hands over there, an older man sitting talking to himself and there was a homeless lady. *'That could be me soon.'* On the way back to my room I asked the Clerk at the front desk.

"May I please have some more coffee up to my room?"

"Of course, I'll send the housekeeper up with a few bags."

The phone was ringing in the room and I had to hurry to open the door to get to the phone. "Hello"

"Hi Hannah, Benson here. I heard about a man, his name is Eric, and he has a room vacancy right now."

I called Eric and he told me that there is single-room vacancy a few blocks from the hotel. *'And how far are a few blocks?'*

There is good news and bad news. The good news is that the room is available now, and the bad news is, I didn't have enough money right then. I calculated the time difference between California and Sweden and called my mother. She was happy to hear from me but when I asked if she had some money to lend me until the end of the month, my mother said,

> "Why don't you ask your father? You know how my money situation is and your father really should help you."

> "What my father should do and what he will do are two different things, mom, and you know that."

We said goodbye and I hung up. I couldn't wait to start my new life. My own life is what I should say! What scared me though is that I don't have any more money until the end of the month, and the month has just started. I almost drove myself crazy thinking about how broke I was and about my situation. I went down to the lobby to borrow the computer to send an email to Merissa. Borrow, by the way, is the wrong word as it cost me $20 to use the computer; $20 that I really couldn't afford to spend.

Now back in my room I had to call my dad, which I already knew wasn't going to be fun, but I didn't have any other choice at this point. The first thing my father asked when I called him was

> "Is everything okay? Have you changed your mind about go back yet?"

> "No I haven't and I am not going too dad." I just couldn't bring myself to ask him for money although I really, really needed it.

> "Dad, I just wonder if I can give you as a reference when looking for a place to stay and when applying for a job?"

"Yes, but….no… that is fine Hannah."

There was hesitation in his voice and I was happy I didn't ask him to help me out with money, or ask if I could borrow some money. *'Hannah you are going to work this out somehow,'* I told myself and I began to feel panic and fearful again. I closed my eyes and fell in a restless sleep.

November 6th 1999

What's the time? Just 6.35 a.m. and I was wide awake. When I sat up in bed, I saw that there was something pushed under the door --my bill. I picked it up but I did not look forward to open it. *'Stop being such a coward Hannah and open it.'* The bill was too high already so there won't be any more phone calls or other extras to put on there. I have to check out today anyway, and prayed that I would have enough money to pay the bill as it is. I called Eric, the man with the single room vacancy, to see if I could go earlier to see the room but he didn't answer. I didn't have any money to give him, but maybe if I tell him my story, my situation, he could take my ring as a deposit until the end of the month. It should be enough.

Just then, it felt as if Eric had my whole future in his hands. Will Eric help me or say no? Once again, I started to panic, but I needed to try to stay calm. I took a deep breath and tried hard to stay focused. Sooner or later, good luck must come to me and I really hope it is today! At 9:00 a.m. I tried to get $340 from the ATM but was denied. So I tried for $300 but was also denied. My eyes quickly filled with tears. I wiped away the tears and thought,' *I'm not going to try again. What if the bank is blocking my card or something.'*

I dragged myself back to the room and was making sure I got all my stuff packed up before it was time to check out. I tried calling Eric again and this time he answered. He gave me the address and told me that I could come and look at the apartment immediately. But before I left, it was time to check out. My little body was shaking and I was scared to even breathe when I gave my card to the clerk at the front desk.

5

"Thank you Ms. Bonde. It will be just a minute." She smiled at me but I didn't smile back. It felt like the longest minute in my life, before she put the slip on the desk and said, "Can you please sign here and here."

I looked at her, so relieved. "Sure, I'll be happy to." At least the hotel got their money but now I was really broke and almost down to my last dollar.

"Can I leave my bags here for a little while? I'm looking for somewhere else to stay."

"Sure, just tell the Bellman and he will take care of them for you."

"Thank you so much."

I grabbed a taxi outside the hotel and gave him the address to where I was going to meet with Eric.

"Excuse me young lady, what are you going to do here?"

"I am looking for a place to stay."

"This neighborhood is dangerous. You should reconsider before you fill out an application. Just my advice."

"Thanks," I said and wished that I would have had a choice, but I will be happy if I get anything.

"Can you please wait for me here and take me back to the hotel when I am done?"

"Yes, I'll wait for you."

It was a small room. It had no furniture but I was willing to take it anyway, anything is better than being homeless. Eric gave me an application and told me it will take a few days to process and even though I needed something right away, I really didn't have any option at this point. I start to fill out the application and got stuck where it said "SSN", I didn't know what that meant so I asked Eric.

"SSN stands for social security number."

"Is SSN the same as the date when you were born?"

Eric smiled and said, "Everyone who is born here in the US or becomes a citizen gets a social security number."

He looked at me again and said, "If you don't have a social security number, there is no need for you to fill out the application. We cannot accept anyone without a social security number. I am sorry Hannah."

"Not as sorry as I am, but thank you anyway." I whispered as I turned my back to him and got in the waiting cab. On the way back to the hotel, my tears start to fall and this time I let them. No room, no money and no hotel! I was officially homeless now. Just like the lady at McDonalds last night, but this is *MY* life. When I got back to the hotel I did my best to put myself together, dry my tears and pretend I was calm, but it was not easy at all. Rita, the hotel manager, tapped me on my shoulder when I came in and asked how it went.

"Not too good."

"You should get The LA Times and look in the classified section, they usually have some things."

Rita was a very sweet woman with dark, thick hair and brown eyes. She spoke with a firm but joyful voice and it reminded me of a teacher talking to her students.

I got the newspaper and called some places but either they were already rented or you needed a social security number. In both cases I would need some money and all I had left was $20 until the end of the month and today is only November 6.

7

Rita passed by where I was standing a couple of times and she looked at me from the corner of her eye. I guess she noticed how stressed I was. Although she was talking to a Black lady when I passed by her, Rita gentle grabbed my arm and asked

"What made you leave Sweden with no money and come to the USA?"
I looked Rita straight in the eyes and it all came tumbling out..

"I ran away from my boyfriend of fourteen and a half years because he tried to kill me …." And I continued, "Jared was abusing me but this time he would kill me if he found me."

Rita's eyes got big while the Black woman took my hand and asked my name? When I told her my name is Hannah she said,

"Hannah, I will pray for you from now on, and I admire how brave you are.
Keep this in mind, 'When you are down to nothing, GOD is up to something.' Good luck with your life."

"Thank you."

When Rita composed herself again from the momentary shock, she said

"Come with me Hannah. I want to talk with you some more."
I followed her out toward the back of the hotel.

"Okay Ms. Bonde, sit down and tell me your story."

And I did. As much as I could in the short amount of time, but I gave Rita details about my life. She was shocked.

"It is horrible that you have to escape, not just country, but your whole family and loved ones because of him." When Rita was done smoking, she tapped my arm, nicked towards the office area, "Come with me."

Rita took me to her office. She made some calls to see if there was anything she could do to help me. No luck there either!

"Did you eat already?"

"No. I haven't, Rita."

"This is the deal Hannah. I am going to pick up some guests at LAX and bring them back to the hotel but after that, I am done for the day. While I'm gone, you wait right here and when I come back, we are going out to dinner and share a bottle of wine. I think you need that." Rita smiled at me.

"I would love to, but I don't have any money Rita."

"I know. But it's on me tonight. Next time it is on you." Rita winked at me and left the room. *'What an amazing woman,'* I thought to myself.

Before we went to dinner, Rita took me to some motels and hostels around the area where the housing was eight to twelve people per room to make it much cheaper. Just to think of sharing a room with so many people made me shake. *'But what other choice do I have?'* What I do know is that I would never feel safe in a place like that.

"Hannah, let's go and eat because I am starving."

First we stopped at the 7-11 store where Rita bought a bottle of white wine for us to take to the restaurant. I was surprised. I had never heard or known that one is allowed to bring your own wine to a restaurant. The restaurant was a little Italian place and we got a table the moment we walked in. Rita was wonderful company and the food was great. So for the first time in months, I was actually enjoying food. We talked about everything but my situation and I told Rita that I thought one of her coworkers was cute.

"I guess you are talking about Tom. He knows he is good looking too. But he doesn't have a good personality. He just looks good."

9

We change the topic and start talking about people's physical outward appearance that may not be very attractive but they can have a heart of gold. I thought to myself *'Yup that must be me because I know I have a very good heart.'* We had a wonderful time and I temporarily forgot about my current state of affairs … that I was really homeless. As I sat there talking to Rita I thought that she is an amazing person, exceptionally kind, and that I just found myself a very good friend. During our talk, Rita told me how much she admired me for making such a bold and brave decision to just get up and leave everything in order to save my life.

> "That was very bold Hannah. I am sure not many people would have done the same thing, made such a drastic change as to leave their home country."

Rita was going to take me to a hostel "down the street" for the night. She said a lot of young people stay there, and the price was reasonable but, I would have to share room. *'How would I be able to sleep when I don't trust anybody? But it's better than to sleep on the streets at least. I got to stay positive.'* We just went passed the hotel where Rita works, when she changed her mind and turned into the driveway of the hotel.

> "I am going to see who the manager is tonight and maybe I can get you a good price for tonight Hannah. Wait here."

Rita talked to the manager in charge and came back out to the car.

> "I got you a room for $15, but only for one night."

Rita said that on Monday she would talk to one of her supervisors to see if they could do anything for me. She said if it wasn't that her roommate was coming home late from work with a friend and that they would probably have a drink before they went to bed, I could have had her couch for the night. Rita walked me up to the room and when it was time for her to leave, I gave her a heartfelt hug and told her how very grateful I was for everything.

> "Get some sleep girl. I'll call you tomorrow."

As soon as Rita left, I lay back down on the bed and I was out – I went right off to sleep mainly because I was very tired from worrying and lack of sleep, but also because of the wine we had at the restaurant. I woke up again around 2:30 a.m. with rap music coming from the McDonalds parking lot. I looked out the window and saw five young Black men playing music on a car radio and dancing in the parking lot. I smiled and said to myself *'Welcome to Cali Hannah'* before I fell asleep again.

November 7th 1999

'I can't breathe, Jared will hear me hiding under the stairs.' I could just reach out and I would be able to touch his leg. *'Please GOD don't let him turn his head and see me.'* My cell phone started to vibrate in my pocket. It scared me half to death. *'Should I answer, no chance, Jared would hear me. Please someone help me.'* I cried in my head. Jared opened the door to the other room. I've got a chance to run, but instead, Jared turns his head and our eyes meet as he looks me straight in the eyes. *'I'm about to die, I'm dying,'* thoughts in my mind as I scared myself awake.

I opened my eyes and looked around. It took me a while to realize that Jared wasn't there. I'm still at the hotel in California!! And I am all by myself. I started to slowly get my breath and pulse rate back to normal. My heart rate slowed down as the fear left me. It was a nightmare, again. *'Thank God, only a nightmare.'*

It was 8:00 a.m. as I turned on the radio to help distract me and shift my focus onto something else. I called my mother and left her a message with the number to the hotel and asked her to please call me back as soon as possible. The phone rang at 10:30 a.m., it was Rita saying, "Do you have any plans for today?" I could hear she was smiling. Rita already knew the answer and without waiting for my answer, she continued,

"It will be checkout time soon. The rate I got for you was just for one night--last night."

"Yeah I know. I am ready to check out already."

"I'm off today and just going to run some errands, so if you want to come with me I can come and pick you up in an hour."

"I would love to go with you Rita," I replied and laughed.

We decided to meet in the lobby 11:30 a.m. As soon as we hung up, I got in the shower and got dressed. Some time later, the phone rang and it was my mother.

"Hi Hannah, how are you?"

"I'm okay mom, but I don't have any more money. Can you call dad to see if he can help me with money? Just for now."

"Why don't you call him yourself Hannah?"

"I just don't want to have to defend or explain my actions all the time." *'And I am not in the mood to have to argue with anybody. No one will understand me anyway and why I did what I did. They weren't the one living in a hell!'* Finally my mother said okay. But I know my mother and she is not going to talk to him, only because she wants to avoid the discussion.
"Mom I will call you again as soon as I can, but for now, there is no way to reach me. OK?"

What I didn't tell her was that as soon as I checked out downstairs. I would be broke and homeless. I didn't have any money left and I was in a foreign country where I don't know anyone or anything. I had a little time before checkout so I organized my suitcase again and then I went down to the lobby, I was hoping my VISA card would go through for the $15 charge for the room. Everyone at the hotel had been so nice and generous to me already.

I checked out before Rita came just in case and yes everything went well. Rita put my suitcase in the back of her Explorer and we left. First we went to a big hardware store where she bought two plants and two blinds and after that she took me down to Venice beach. It was amazing. She bought us lunch and there were some people who performed on the boardwalk. There were homeless people sleeping on boxes or just standing around. *'What am I going to do? I need to find a solution of my homeless situation but right now; I just want to enjoy the sun and Rita's company.'*

She took me down to the ocean and I had never seen a beach like that before. I felt like a little girl who is seeing the beauty of the world for the very first time. I guess I am in one way. We left and went to Rita's house to drop of the things she bought, but while there we changed into shorts and T-shirts. I had to borrow some from Rita as all I had was winter clothes. After we had changed, it was time to plant her purchases. We stayed at Rita's house and I got introduced to her roommate Danny, who was late for work so he just said,

"Hello Hannah, nice to meet you. I'll catch you guy's later."

I washed my clothes there while Rita made us some dinner and she said I could stay in their house for the night. Both Danny and Rita had to work in the morning, but she said I could either stay in their house or Danny could take me to work with him for a few hours so I could see what Beverly Hills was like. Danny worked at a hotel just like Rita so he would be in Beverly Hills anyway. We continued to talk about what my options were, and what I could do. Perhaps talk to a women's shelter here and see if they would be willing to take me in.

Rita said she would talk to her mother, Alyssa, and see if she had any ideas of what to do or where to turn. She gave me a pillow and a blanket so that I could make my bed on the couch.

It was getting late and Rita needed to get to bed as she had to get up early the next morning. We said good night and I told Rita how grateful I was. When I was alone in the living room and was about to go to sleep I promised myself, *'one day when I got myself together, I will show Rita how much her helping me is appreciated'*, and I fell asleep as soon as my head touched the pillow.

The morning after Rita woke me up at 9:00 a.m. before she left so I could get ready. I took a shower, put on some makeup, before it was time for Danny to get ready for work. We left the house around 10:40 a.m. When we got to the hotel where Danny works, he started to introduce me to his coworkers. "This is my new friend Hannah and she is from Sweden." Everyone was so nice to me. Danny asked if I wanted to eat lunch there at the hotel or he could give me money so I could eat someplace else. But I said the hotel was fine. Then Danny called George who works in security and asked him to take me down to the cafeteria?

"Sure, my pleasure"

We went down to the cafeteria and George gave the chef a food coupon that he had gotten from Danny to pay for my meal. Talk about wonderful people! The cafeteria was buffet style which amazed me. George said,

"I would love to keep you company but I have to go back to work for now."

I think I'd been there for fifteen minutes when George came back with his lunch and I was happy to see someone I knew. It felt as if the other people were staring at me and I was feeling uncomfortable. George asked if I was here on vacation but I said

"No I moved here from Sweden."

"Wow, so how long have you been here?"
"Four days."

"Why did you move?"

"I just needed to get a life, my own life." I explained to him a little about how I had to run away from Sweden.

"You seem to be a very bright and nice person so I'm sure everything will come together and turn out okay for you."

It was nice to hear. George had to leave again after taking me back to Danny. Danny then sends me to the shopping mall in the hotel limousine and gave me a telephone number to call when I was ready to be picked up. This was my first time in a limo and I felt like Julia Roberts in *Pretty Woman.*

I still only had twenty dollars left so I window shopped. I was excited and amazed at all the nice things I saw. I ended up walking from Century City, back to the hotel. On the way back, I stopped at Starbuck's and had a coffee. Danny was surprised that I had walked all the way back and asked why I didn't call him for the car. I had to explain that after being a prisoner in my home for so long, I was happy to feel free and didn't mind to walk, in fact I enjoyed the freedom to walk out in the open.

Rita came home at just about the same time as Danny and me. We, I mean he had bought some beer and white wine to have with our dinner while we watched Monday night football. Rita went to bed early while Danny and I stayed up talking until 2:00 a.m. I thanked him very much for his generosity. We said good night and Danny went into his room and I fell asleep on "my" couch.

In the morning Rita came to tell me that she didn't feel well so she was staying home from work today. She asked if she could have a word with me?

"Of course," I said.

"Hannah, do you have any plans of what to do or where to go from here?"
"No nothing. But I'll figure something out Rita. Don't worry."

"I can't promise anything Hannah, but if you like I can ask Danny if you can stay with us for two weeks and help us out with some rent?"

"I don't have any money at all right now. I won't get any money until the end of the month Rita."

"I know, but don't worry about it. You can pay us when you get your money."

"I'd love to stay here if Danny says it's okay. What would I do without you Rita?"

"You would be just fine Hannah. I have no doubts at all about that."

It was a very generous offer, but I still need to find a room, a place where I can sleep and put my things but I don't know how because I am broke. I just don't want to force myself into anyone's life. But I will, I will pay them back and that as soon as I can.

I called my mother to see if she had reached my father, but my mother said no. Honestly, I don't even know if she tried.

"Did you try to call his cell phone?" My father always answers on his cell phone.

"No, I didn't. I don't have his cell phone number." *'You can just ask Annie or me for it,'* but instead I said, "Let me give it to you mom."

I promised to write her. I told mom I had some new and very helpful friends here with whom I would be staying for a couple of weeks. She asked about them but I said I would tell her later. The less mom and dad knows, the better.

Rita, Danny and I went out to get something to eat and stopped at a Mexican restaurant which was just around the corner from the house. The food was great and we all went to bed early that night.

This morning I again woke up from a nightmare. I was emotionally drained and exhausted. I was dreaming that Jared got a hold on my VISA card and had cleaned out my bank account when my money came in and I didn't know what to do.

Jared really has brain washed me and caused me to be so fearful. But I need to pull myself together and to stay strong. I have to realize my life has changed and Jared cannot tell me what to do anymore. We are not even in the same country, damn it!

I heard when Rita left for work and knew she would not be home for dinner tonight because she had a business dinner to attend. Danny woke up and before he left to run errands, he said he would take me out to a late lunch when he got back. After he left and I was by myself, I got the broom and started to do a little tidying up of the house. I thought, *'at least this is something I can do for Rita and Danny to show them I appreciate their kindness and generosity.'*

I called my mom again; she had now talked to dads' wife Liza who told mom that dad would need a telephone number where they could reach me before he would do anything to help me. *'Great! But I'll have to ask Rita if I can give out her number.'*

I called Rita at work and explained the situation and told her that my father said he would need a phone number to reach me before he would even think of helping me.

"Give them the phone number Hannah."

"Are you sure?"

"Please do."

I called my mom back and gave her the telephone number. I really didn't want them to know anything about where I was staying or how to reach me in case of Jared got a hold on that information. Frankly I didn't trust Liza, or any of them really. Seems like none of them understand how serious this is and Liza can be very ignorant. Even if I told them not to tell Jared, one of them might do it anyway. Maybe by mistake but anyway!

Right after I hung up with my mom, my dad and Liza called me back. My father started to ask me questions and I tried to avoid giving him specific answers.

"Where are you and who are you with?"

"I am staying with some people I met at the hotel."

"So what are your plans Hannah? I'm not going to support you."

17

"I don't expect you to support me dad. I am going to stay here and get a job."

"Do you have a VISA to stay in the country?"

"Yes I do, but it is only valid for three months."

"And then what Hannah?

"I don't know dad but I'm already here."

"You don't have any papers to work and you can't stay in the country without a VISA. The US will be extremely hard on you if they find out you are there without a VISA and you are working. You will be in trouble with the law Hannah. You need to go back to Sweden and get your papers right. Then you can go back if you want to. If you don't do this the right way, I won't help you."

I knew all these things my father was telling me were Liza's words not his.

"Dad you don't need to help me if you don't want to, but I am not going back, no matter what. I can't! I'd never survive."

My father was going to think about it and he would let me know if I could borrow some money, but he couldn't give me an answer just then. We hang up and now all I can do is wait. At least I had asked him to help.

Danny came home and we went to Santa Monica pier for lunch. It was really supper as it was already 5 o'clock. We had Mexican food and walked along the pier afterwards. The ocean was so fascinating and beautiful with the moonlight reflected in the water. I felt so free. I looked towards the city and saw all the streetlights and tall buildings and just a short distance away was the beach right under the pier. It was so peaceful.

On the way back to the house Danny and I talked about what kind of jobs I had in Sweden. I told him that,

"I drove a city bus for a while, worked as a cashier at a gas station and I also drove a taxicab."

"Are you kidding me? You, a bus driver?

I looked seriously at Danny.

"What's wrong with that? You don't think I can handle a big bus, huh?"

I smiled. Danny could not believe that I've been a city bus driver, when I was as short as I am. It was fun. Danny asked a lot about Sweden and my ex Jared so I told him. We got back to the house and I went straight to bed but before I went to sleep, I thought how lucky I was to have found two so nice and wonderful friends. *'Everything will be great Hannah.'*

Already November 11 and when it was time for Danny to leave for work, he asked if I wanted to go with him to Beverly Hills or just stay here, around the house.

"I'm staying here. I need some time by myself." I've been here for a week and I need to figure out what to do, what my next step is going to be.

After Danny left for work, I went out and started to walk down the boulevard towards the beach and I passed a hair salon with a "Help Wanted" sign in the window. I went in and the girl asked me for a social security number. *Again?* I didn't have one, that meant I couldn't even apply for the job. Guess I have to look for something else. I was out for two hours and there was so much to see. *'One day I will get my own car and need to know my way around.'*

Rita called to ask me to feed the cats, and when she got home around 7:30 p.m. we had dinner. For dessert, we had coffee and pie while watching TV. Rita fell asleep on the couch but after a brief nap she woke up and went to her room so I could make my bed on the couch. I heard when Danny came home, but he walked straight to his room and I fell asleep.

I woke up when Rita left for work at just about 7:00 a.m. I tried to go back to sleep but it was impossible. My thoughts went back to how my life used to be in Sweden. The fear I had and still have of Jared. *'Why can't I just erase my past?'*

The phone rang and it was my mother, who called just to tell me that she wanted to hear my voice. I told her that I needed to find another place to stay and a job so I can make money enough to take care of myself. I don't want to stay at Rita's and Danny's and overstay my welcome, or to start getting on their nerves. Their friendship means too much to me. It seems as if they both enjoy my company and having me in the house right now and I want to keep it that way.

I got up and did the dishes, ironed and cleaned up whatever there was to clean up. It feels real good for me to do something for Rita and Danny. I am so grateful for everything they do for me. Then I took a shower, got dressed and put on some makeup, just some mascara and eyeliner, which makes me feel a little brighter and uplifted.

When Danny came home, we went to the shopping center and a place called Jamba Juice. We got our drinks, some kind of fruit juice, and then we went down to the Marina. Some parts reminded me of Puerto Banus in Spain. That's where my father lived. But Marina Del Ray was bigger while Puerto Banus was more luxurious.

When we stood there by the channel while the boats were coming in, it started to feel like I was on vacation and that I would need to go back to prison soon. I caught myself in that negative thought and said *'no Hannah, you are not going back anymore. You are here to stay forever and you have the freedom to do whatever you want to do.'* I was overwhelmed by how nice it was to have a life where I can make my own decisions. Do what I want and have my own beliefs.

Rita came home right after we got back home and the three of us went out to dinner. We talked about my situation and Danny said

"If there is anyone who can help you to get things right, it's Rita."

That showed me how much he looked up to her, and also how lucky and blessed I am having met her. Their neighbor Debbie stopped by and had a drink with us at the restaurant. Rita rode home with her and I rode back home with Danny. I asked him if Rita had said anything about my staying there or that she didn't want me to stay there and Danny said

"No she has not, but Rita told me how much she likes you."

That was nice to hear. I told Danny that I like Rita too, she is so nice. "In the matter of fact, I like both of you."

November 13th 1999

Rita's TV woke me up but I fell asleep again. When I woke up again it was already 11:30 a.m. and it was time to get up. I made myself some coffee and started to write again. Unusual, huh? Honestly, I can't define how I feel, because everything seems to be so surreal. As if I'm in a dream and will wake up and be back in the nightmare I lived in Sweden. I need to get it in my head, in my being, in my mind really that this is what reality is now! I am not in Sweden and Jared can no longer control me.

Rita, Danny and I stayed in and just hung around the house all day. We ordered pizza for dinner and watched "Ghost" on TV. I love that movie but it is so sad and as always makes me cry. Rita went off to sleep and my attention, once again went to how blessed I was to know Rita and Danny. They treat me as if I came here to visit them, showing me around and taking me places I would never see if it wasn't for them. I hope our friendship will last even when I move because Rita and Danny will always have a special place in my heart. They have been so very helpful to me.

I again woke up really early from another nightmare where Jared was chasing me and I tried to hide from him. It was the same as the last nightmare where I woke up right when our eyes met. Jared saw me and I knew it was over. I can't breathe when I wake up. It is a horrible feeling. *'Breathe Hannah you are safe,'* I had to keep repeating to myself. *'When are these nightmares going to stop?!'* I got up and made some coffee, and Rita came in and asked me

"Hey Hannah, I need to go to Home Depot and get some pots for my plants.
Do you want to come with me?"

"Of course. I don't have anything better to do, anyway." I smiled at her.

We went to that big hardware store, bought the plants and some pots. After that, it was back home and we planted the flowers and put them on the porch by the door. They turned out so nice with the dark pink flowers and green leafs. We got back into the car after we were done and went to the shopping center to get some food for dinner and then back to the house.

Rita and I talked about my plans and what I'm going to do? I felt the pressure coming on. *'She doesn't want me here,'* I thought again. Rita didn't say that but I could feel it and I don't like that feeling. But I do understand. Rita is sheltering a complete stranger in her house, someone who sleeps on her couch and on top of that, Rita is supporting me too. That is quite a lot to bear for a stranger.

I picked up the LA Times and looked at places for rent and also for jobs. I can't afford anything big and it can't be too expensive. There were a few that seemed to fit what I wanted. I will call them tomorrow. I went to bed around midnight and I felt the anxiety grow within me.

Thanksgiving 1999

Rita had plans on Thanksgiving, Thursday 25th. She was going to serve food to the homeless people downtown, and she asked if I wanted to go with her. Yes of course I do, and I was looking forward to it.

Rita's family was going to meet at her mother's house on Wednesday, the 24th to celebrate Thanksgiving. She had told her mother Alyssa about my situation and asked if she had any suggestions of what I could. I had never met Rita's family, but her mother told her that she doesn't like that Rita has a complete stranger living with her. Therefore, it surprised me when Rita said,

> "Hannah, I just spoke with my mother today and she invited you to the Thanksgiving dinner as well. You want to come with me?"

"Yes thank you. That is so sweet of her."

So on Wednesday morning, the 24th, we headed for Rita's mother's house in the Valley. Rita drove for one hour and when we were almost there, Rita stopped at a condominium complex and there were a little lake in the middle of the complex. I sat down on the stairs and told Rita that I am going to live like this, by a lake one day.

"Take a picture please," and I gave her a smile.

Back in the car for just a few more minutes and we arrived to Rita's mom's house. As Rita and I walked in, everyone turned towards us as Rita announced 'Hey everyone, we are here,' and introduced me around to her mother, sisters, their husbands, nieces and nephews. Everyone was helping with the cooking, doing dishes, setting the table etc, and they even put me to work which made me happy and I felt so accepted.

When it was time to leave, all of the family members told me it was so nice meeting me, and it was definitely my pleasure meeting them. I had touched their hearts too. Just like they and Rita had touched mine, also.

December 1ˢᵗ, I can't believe it.' The time was flying and the new millennium was getting closer so fast. *'What am I going to do with my life? I need a job and a place for myself.'*

I again was beginning to feel stressed. Just thinking about my situation made me feel anxious. I sure won't accomplish anything by lying in bed the whole day. I got up, got ready and walked up to the market at the corner to get the LA Times. Once back in the house, I made a cup of coffee and started to look for jobs in the Classified. I have to be very careful when I call but at the same time, I have to tell them I don't have a permit to work in the US, because if it's totally out of question, I don't want to waste both their and my time.

One of the ads I called was Global café in Santa Monica, and I got to talk to the owner himself. His name was Retek. I told him I was from Sweden and when I told him about my "legal" situation he said "Come here tomorrow and we'll talk about it and see what we can do." I was so excited when I hung up I had to make the effort to calm myself down before I was going to meet with him tomorrow. Both Rita and Danny were very happy for me and wished me good luck.

On December 2ⁿᵈ, Rita woke me up before she left for work and told me that I had until Sunday to find somewhere else to stay. I had stayed with them for almost a month. I could not fault her for asking me to leave. Remember, she had met me, housed me and fed me for a month having not ever seen or even heard of me before then. Rita was being nice about it but I knew it was getting to her that I hadn't found either a job or a place to live.

I got ready and left to catch the bus to Santa Monica where the café was located. I got there an hour early and had something to eat at McDonald's before I walked over to Global Café to meet with Retek. After meeting with him he promised to give me a chance and I was very happy. I would get a few days training and if all went well then Retek would hire me. I could start my training the same night, the shift starting at 6.45 p.m. to 10:00 p.m. My first night went very well and I had a good feeling about the job. I am very friendly and I am easy to talk too as well as to talk to people and have, most of my working life, worked in service to others.

The following day, I had the late shift from 9:00 p.m. to 2:00 a.m. I was just happy to be doing something, something for myself. I got to work 8.10 p.m. and Keith with whom I worked the day before, was happy to see me and gave me a coffee. I watched to learn how the other servers did their routines and handled customers because I wanted to be good at my job as quickly as possible. Retek arrived at about 8.30 p.m. and he got angry when he saw me there.

"You are here too early. If you are going to disrespect my time schedules, you can leave."

I couldn't believe it; Retek fired me because I was at work too early! I said goodbye to Keith and he asked why I was leaving. I told him what Retek told me. Keith got very upset and told Retek "I quit too, if you let her go." Retek didn't change his mind, so both Keith and I walked out and left him there by himself.

"You didn't have to do that," I told Keith when we walked to his car.

"I know but you don't treat people like that. That's just not fair. Can I give you a ride home?"

"Sure if it's not too much trouble."

Keith dropped me off and wished me good luck with everything. Rita and Danny were both surprised to see me back so early. During dinner Rita again told me that I still had to find a place and move out. I said I understood and appreciated everything they did for me. Danny got upset with her and said,

"I live here too and think Hannah can stay here until she finds a place, something decent."

25

"It's okay Danny. I'll figure something out. The two of you have already done more than enough for me."

The last thing I wanted was for them to argue about me. I'll definitely do my best to find something.

Courage to call

I went to my journal for comfort and started to write. I just let my thoughts flow. It was getting closer to the holidays and I was thinking about how different this Christmas will be from all the others. Then I thought about Pauli and Ron's family. I hadn't talked to them since that time I called them from the Women's Shelter. They had no idea where I was. The Svenssons don't even know I left Sweden. I was thinking about the kids and I started to cry and my heart was aching. I knew the whole family was hurt by not knowing what happened to me, but I have been too scared to trust them. Maybe not to trust them, but it was the same with the Svenssons as it was with my family. What is that saying, "You can't say by mistake what you don't know."

After all, it is *Jareds* sister and her family. I didn't know if I had the right to put that burden on them, where they would know where I was but they couldn't tell him.

I really didn't want to cause disruption in their lives. I decided that there was just one thing I could do, and it was to call them and see how things went from there. If I called, at least Pauli and the rest of her family would know I was okay, well relatively okay. Then I could leave it up to them if they wanted to maintain contact with me.

It was morning here in Los Angeles and early evening in Sweden when I dialed the number. I was so nervous my hands were shaking. The Svenssons' hadn't heard anything from me in about two months. Jay answered the phone.

"Hey Jay, it's aunty Hannah."

I could hear him take a deep breath as he said, "Hey aunty, how are you?"

"I'm okay Jay, how are you guys doing?"
"We are okay, but we miss you aunty."

My eyes got teary and the tears started to fall. It took all my strength to keep Jay from hearing that I was crying.

"Is your mom home?"

"No she isn't, but she'll be home soon, in an hour or so."

"Okay, I'll call back then. Can you tell your mom that I called?"

"I sure will. We miss you aunty."

We hung up and I called them back after about ninety minutes. Pauli answered the phone and when she heard my voice, we both started to cry.

"How are you Hannah and where are you? One day everything was fine and you were here and the next thing we know, you're just gone and we don't even know if you are dead or alive."

"I'm okay but I had to leave. If I had stayed Pauli, I would be dead now. I didn't mean to just leave you without telling you, but Jared is your brother and your kid's uncle. They adore him. I don't want to talk bad about him so the children get a bad picture of him. I don't even know what he has told you."

"First Jared just said that you had left him, but not what had happened. We didn't ask either as we know how Jared can be. But a few days later Jared explained to us, he said "Hannah left because I haven't been really nice to her.""

"Not really nice!?. That is so typically!"

27

"Hannah, do you want to tell me what really happened?"

"He kidnapped me and held me locked in our apartment, abusing me so badly I thought he'd kill me…. one more day and he would have!"

We continued talking and I told her a little more of what had happen and why I left. I told her I had been to two different Women 's Shelters in Sweden, and that Jared found me at the first one. That I knew then thI had to leave and leave very, very soon. It was just a matter of time before Jared would find me again and at that time, I wouldn't be able to escape. I'd be dead! Pauli asked why I didn't come and stay with them. Jared would never have bothered me with Ron there Pauli said.

But I know that Jared would have one way or another. He would never have left me alone as long as he knew where I was and I didn't want to get them or anyone else involved.

"I didn't even know if you would want to have anything to do with me after I left your brother Pauli?"

"Hannah don't be silly! You have and will always be my sister and our kids aunty. Our boys have grown up with you and we all love you as much as we love him. Yes, Jared is my flesh and blood but you are my soul sister."

It was so nice to talk to Pauli and she said it felt like a stone fell from her heart now that she knew I was okay.

Around the same time I disappeared, Pauli had gotten sick and as she understood what was going on between Jared and me, it made her sick from worrying about me too. I gave Pauli my cell phone number so they could reach me. I knew now that they would never give it to Jared. The Svenssons knew that Jared had treated me badly, but they didn't know the half of it, or how bad it really was. Pauli was right. They are my family too. When we hung up, I felt some comfort to know that they still wanted me in their life.

Merissa (my Swedish friend) had e-mailed me the address to a Norwegian Seaman's Church that was not too far from Los Angeles. Maybe I could turn to them if I needed help, Merissa said.

A few days later, I called the church and spoke with Anna, the Swedish priest's wife and she told me I was more than welcome to visit at any time. I decided to rent a car a few days before New Year's Eve and headed south from Rita's to the church. I was nervous having not been in a church for a long time, for many years. I found my way quite easily and found parking right outside of the church building. As soon as I entered the church, a tall man came to introduce himself and wish me welcome. His name was Mike and he was the Swedish priest. Mike showed me around and he asked what made me come to the states. While I was talking with Mike, Anna joined us. Shortly thereafter Mike had to leave and I ended up telling Anna my whole life story about my past and the reason I had to escape to the US and far from Sweden. She was stunned and amazed, almost speechless by my story but she promised to be on the lookout for any job opportunities. Then she remembered,

> "Actually, there was someone who called me yesterday and she was looking for a nanny. I have her phone number somewhere in the office. I'll be right back."

Anna came back and handled me a telephone number and told me that I should call right away before the woman finds someone else, and that I could use their office telephone. I called right then but there was no answer so I left my name and cell phone number on the answering machine.

A new millennium and a new life

It was December 31st 1999, I had been in the US almost 2 months and started to get used to the idea that I was actually living here in Los Angeles. What better time to start my new life than now. Not just New Year's Eve, but the New Millennium –2000! I feel so ready to get a job and a new start. To build a new life, Hannah's own life! I was so excited and couldn't wait for this millennium to begin. My mother called and we wished each other Happy New Year. I never thought, in my wildest dream that I would be away from my family on such a big occasion.

Six months ago I thought Jared and I were going to celebrate the Millennium together and plan for our upcoming wedding which was going to be May 6, 2000 if things had stayed the same. *'I can't believe that I actually was going to marry him! A man who was killing me slowly but surely by his beatings, obsession to constantly control me and everything I did.'*

I remembered when I was a little girl how I used to dream about a wonderful big wedding with me in a beautiful white dress that was right above my knees in the front with a long train behind, and a wonderful man dressed in a nice tuxedo. We would love each other so much and everything would be perfect, just like the fairy tale. That's what all girls want, I guess ... but I realized a long time ago that it would not happen with Jared. At that point though, I was too scared to leave him.

What saved me, a miracle in tragedy, was when I broke my ankle on July 11, 1999 and the doctor told me that I was not to do anything but sit still and relax to allow the ankle to heal. That is when I got the chance to review my life and I was honest with myself. I saw that Jared hadn't changed, that I was the one that had changed. I wasn't pushing the limits with him anymore. I now knew when Jared was revving up and heading, like a runaway train, toward derailment and him being out of control. I was now aware of his moods and now in control, somewhat. I knew when to be quiet. That was my way of protecting myself from being beaten, I was now aware that that was the only way for me.

I realized that I only had two choices -- that I was either going to marry him and live a life in fear of being controlled and beaten just for being me, and Jared would likely kill me at a young age, or that I would leave him and also have to leave the country. Therefore, my choice was an easy one, one of self-survival, when I thought ahead and saw how my life would be with him, married or not. But how to put this plan into motion? I had to plan, figure and scheme to do everything by myself, and in secret.

"Hannah what do you say? Pasta sounds good huh?"

"What Rita?"

She looked at me from the corner of her eye, smiled and asked

"Where were you?"
"Oh, back in Sweden with my crazy ex," I answered without a smile.

"Hannah you are here now and you just started a new life. Enjoy it."

"Yeah you're right. New year, new beginning in a new country. That works!"

That got me smiling. *'I just have to let my past go and never look back again, which is easier said than done.'*

I called my father and as soon as he answered the phone, I could hear he was drunk. But I also sensed something else in his voice that I had never heard before. I heard fear and my father was crying. I was afraid and scared and I felt a shiver run through my body from my head to my toes. With as calm a tone as I could muster, I asked
"Dad what's wrong? Why are you crying?"

"Hannah I don't feel well and I miss my boys so much."

I thought for a second. "Where are the boys dad?"

"Liza took the boys away from me and went to Sweden. She did not even tell me Hannah."

"Oh my God. Are you OK, dad?"

31

"Don't worry about me, think of yourself now. Listen to me Hannah and listen carefully. I want you to listen to what other people tell you, but always remember, only you know what is best for you. You are a very smart girl. You have always known the difference between right and wrong and I trust that you will make the right decisions in life. You always have. Don't let anyone tell you what to do or not to do. I am so proud of you and I love you Hannah."

Quietly my tears fell and rolled down my cheeks and left a salty taste on my lips before dropped into my lap.

"I love you too dad. If you only knew how much it means to me to hear you say that I have all your trust. Happy New Year, dad."

"You too Hannah, Happy New Year. I love you."

I was still crying when we hang up. I have been waiting all my life to hear my father tell me that he was proud of me and now he had. The sadness I felt, knowing my father was all by himself on New Year's Eve was incredible. Alone in their big house with the white tile, dark wood in the kitchen and red/yellow striped curtains over the big windows in the living room. My father was probably sitting out by the pool, a drink in his hand and looking out over the city from the mountains where the house was located and feeling empty and lost.

I felt like another piece of the puzzle of my life had found its place. I know this will be a great millennium. From now on, I will speak up about my opinions and what is on my mind. I will listen and follow my father's advice.

Danny worked until 1:00 a.m. and Rita and I were home watching New Year's celebration on TV all around the world. My phone rang and it was Chrystal from Van Nuys, the woman whom I had called from the church's office as she was looking for a nanny. Chrystal said,

"I'm not sure how much help I really need, because I am home with our son Aaron, who is two and a half, but when I go back to work we will need someone. But maybe we can be friends? I don't have too many friends here and no Swedish friends. I would love to meet for a coffee, lunch or something and I can show you around." Without giving me a chance to answer, Chrystal continued, "How about the next two weeks?"

"Sure I would love to."

I was happy and I needed as many contacts as possible, either work or friends. I had to start somewhere.

Rita and I had a relaxing dinner with some wine and small talk. "I really don't like to go out on New Year's Eve. There is always some mishap on New Year's with someone is out playing with guns instead of fireworks," Rita said. That wasn't common in Sweden, but this is the US and it is different here. I should stop comparing everything and get used to how it is here in the US because this is now my country, my home from now on.

Danny called at midnight and wished us a Happy New Year. When he came home around 2.30 a.m., it was time for the three of us to toast with champagne and I start by saying; "Toast for a new friendship that will last forever and thank you both for everything. I love you guys."

Rita went to her room while Danny and I were up talking about the evening and all the celebrations. He had seen some of them while at work. When Danny went to his room, I could hear them arguing and I felt it was my fault. Even though I knew I hadn't done anything wrong I felt the pressure to move as soon as possible so we would remain friends. I didn't want to cause anyone any problems, argument or unhappiness. I just wanted them both to be happy. *'A new year, a new beginning and a new life is here, just waiting for me,'* was the last thing on my mind before I fell asleep the morning of January 1, 2000.

A new millennium and a new life

The new millennium started out great but I was tired from last night. Once again, I was thinking how happy I was not to have problems with alcohol or drugs, especially after everything I had been through in my past. Now it's a new year and a new millennium so it is time for me to get my act together and make some plans for my future. I had some interviews scheduled and there were ads ever day in LA Times for nanny positions. One thing I had learned since I came to the US is that without a social security number or a working Visa, you are very limited with what you can do in this country, but I can't let that stop me from building my own life here.

I had been through hell and back to get here. I knew it wouldn't be easy, but no one said life would be easy. After talking to my father I knew I had his trust and support, this millennium belongs to me.

It was six days into the New Year when I met with Chrystal for the first time. She and her son Aaron came to pick me up at Rita's and we went down to Manhattan Beach and strolled around at the pier. We started to talk as soon as I got into the car. Chrystal was so easy to talk to. She has lived in the US for ten years, she's married and has one child. I felt comfortable with her and it was like we had known each other for a long time. The only thing I avoided talking about was the reason why I came to the US. I'm so suspicious of everyone but I made the effort to trust her.

I've learned that you have got to give to get, so I did my best. I told Chrystal how I met Rita and Danny and how we had affected each other's life in a positive way. She told me that I definitely should go to the DMV and get a Driver License before my Tourist Visa expired because that would help me. I was open to all advice. Chrystal also said she'd help me with everything if I needed any help.

It was getting late so Chrystal took me back home and we decided to spend some more time together the coming Saturday. This was the beginning of the friendship between Chrystal and me, which would grow stronger than any friendship I have had in a long time.

The following day, I called an advert about a South Bay nanny position. I spoke with Sue who told me that they live six months in California and the other six months in Hawaii where the family had another estate. She wanted me to come for an interview later that day and Rita drove me there. I was very surprised when I saw Sue's big house which was right on the beach, perhaps about 8000 square feet. The house was luxurious and reminded me of my father's house in Marbella, Spain, but more contemporary. The interior was wood and tile, very nice and clean and had a personal touch that made it feel warm and inviting. I'd love to work here and Sue seemed to be a nice woman. She said she had two Swedish nannies before and liked the fact I was from Sweden, as she had good experiences with the other two girls.

However, there were two issues. First, I didn't have a car or driver license and second, I didn't have any experience with this type of job. She would have to talk with her husband and get back to me.

A few days later, I got a phone call from Sue who had talked to her husband and they both had agreed and wanted me to come down for the following weekend to meet the kids and Stephan, her husband, and of course she would pay me for the weekend she added. If everything went well and they decided to hire me, they would figure out to handle the car issue. To get experience we all need to start somewhere Sue said. I would try out over the weekend and see how everything went with the kids and see if I qualified for the position.

When I met with Chrystal that Saturday, she took me over to her house in the Valley. Her house was a three-bedroom Spanish style house, light warm colors but still elegant. Chrystal definitely knew how to put things together and make it a home. We spent the whole day together. We had lunch by a lake in the mountains and afterwards we went back to her house. While we talked I told her about my life and the reason I had to leave Sweden.

"I had to get away from a crazy man."

I recall Chrystal saying,
> "Hannah there is a lot of crazy people here in California as well."

"I know Chrystal. But here is no one particular whom chasing me."

I looked out over their little backyard where almost all the grass had turned yellow. Once again, I felt a sting in my heart when I reminisce on what I had been through these past fifteen years. I continued to tell Chrystal how much I had to sacrifice to save my life. I was still hurt and there was so much pain and emotional baggage that I had to deal with. I was quiet for a moment before I turn to Chrystal and said with a smile, "But it was definitely worth it."

Chrystal told me that she was depressed after the birth of her son. She missed her family in Sweden and it was hard to find real friends over here. Her tears start falling from my story and her own emotions. I told her it's nothing wrong feeling the way she does.

"You can't control how you feel but the most important thing is how you deal with it."

I still think about Jared and wished that we would have been able to work out our situation and go our separate ways and on good terms, but there was no way that was possible. So I just had to deal with the situation as it is. There are times when I still cry just thinking about the last week with him. That last week I was at home and how Jared treated me and beat me so badly. But through all that I am glad to be alive.

"I will do whatever it takes to get my life back on the right track," I told Chrystal and she responded,

"If there is anything, anything, I can do to help you, just let me know."

We both needed someone, a friend to lean on. We found each other exactly at the right time. Chrystal told me,

"It's so hard for me to believe how a strong woman like you Hannah, has been through such a dreadful thing."

"I know, but all that matters now is that I am here and I am alive."

We talked about what was important for me to do now that I was going to live here and Chrystal said, 'First of all, you need to go and get you a social security number and take a Driver License because it will make your life so much easier.'

Glad for the advice I got but when I got to the social security office, the lady asked me why I needed one.

"I need to open a bank account." But now the lady told me with an attitude,

"You don't need a social security number to open a bank account, to buy a car or even to buy a house in Beverly Hills. I'm sorry but we can't give you one."

It was a setback for me and I start to feel discouraged again. *'Why is this happening to me? But I won't let this stop me from building my own life here.'* Next stop was the DMV. I filled out the papers for a CDL and when the clerk asked for my social security number, I got quiet for a second but pulled myself together and told her.

"I haven't got it yet." She accepted that answer and gave me all the papers to fill out.

'Maybe I just should try to take a written test while I'm here.' I did but I failed. There were words I didn't even know what they meant. *'Okay I got to be more patient with myself,'* so I grabbed a book and went back to the house. At least this is something that I can learn so I'll pass but when it comes to a social security number, I just have to let it go.

The following Friday, Sue came to pick me up to take me to her house for the weekend. Suddenly an old feeling of insecurity came over me. To be away from Rita and Danny where I felt safe, but I better get used to it. It's the first time since I moved in with them that Rita and Danny actually will have a whole weekend alone without me.

Sue and I dropped my weekend bag in their huge house on the beach before we went to pick up her daughter Shelly from preschool. When Sue and I got there and Shelly saw us, to our surprise she came running to me and gave me a big hug. She didn't hug her mother. Shelly was an adorable little girl and she was talking to me like she had known me forever. Later that day I also got a chance to meet Rob, her son who was six, and Stephan, her husband.

That evening I went to the pier and had a drink by myself for the first time. It felt a little weird to be there all alone, but I also felt calmer than I have been in a long time. It was just me, myself and I. On my way back to their house, walking on the Strand, my thoughts went back to Thanksgiving when we were at Rita's mother's house and Rita showed me some nice condos up in Calabasas, and the picture of me in front of that nice lake and on the picture I'd written "this is me in front of my new house".

'If I get this job, I won't be living by a lake but by the ocean, right on the beach.' I went to bed early and it was so quiet, and the bed was so big. It was a California king size bed I had all to myself. I was laying there and even though I felt lonely, I was at peace. *'I can do this. It will be just great,'* I said to myself.

The rest of the weekend was easy and we went back and forth with play dates, birthday party, ballet classes, babysitting while Sue and Stephan went on their weekly date. Sue let me drive, as she wanted to evaluate my driving skills. Well if there is anything I'm good at and have the confidence to know I'm good at, it is how to drive. At night, I gave the kids a bath and put them in bed without any trouble. We all got along very well. Sue even asked if I could stay an extra day and when she drove me back, she told me the position was mine if I wanted it.

"Hannah I don't need any more time to think. I knew on Friday when we went to pick up Shelly and she embraced you, even though she had never met you. Children instinctively know when they meet someone who is genuine."

I just couldn't believe it; I got a job, going to have my own studio here in Hermosa Beach and in Hawaii, and on top of all that I will make money. I was so happy!

It was time for me to take my test at DMV on January 18th. I was worried about the written test because of the language but now after studying the booklet, I had a little more confidence than before. I can't afford to fail this time and I need my driver license now when I'm about to start working. I had a rental car and everything was great, until I came to DMV and the lady at the desk told me I needed someone with me who is over 18 and has a CDL.

"Are you kidding me? Why didn't they tell me that earlier?"

"I don't know, but I'll give you 30 minutes to find someone," the lady behind the counter said.

I felt how the stress tried to get to me, but I had to stay calm. *'Think Hannah, think. You got to figure something out.'* Well I had nothing to lose so I asked the older woman who were standing behind me in line and she agreed to do it. I was so grateful and once again, I thanked God for blessing me. I passed the test easily now that I understood the words. I only missed one question, and when I walked out from DMV with the permit in my hand I felt like I had just won the lottery.

The day after, January 19th at 10 am, Sue and Shelly came and picked me up to take me to my new "home" and my new job. I was so excited and at the same time sad to leave Rita and Danny. I was scared because those two had become to be my "family", my security since I came here to the states. Rita and Danny will always have a special place in my heart and we are going to be friends forever. How many people would take in a stranger, let them stay with them for 2.5 months and take that person under their wings like Rita and Danny had done with me? Not too many, not many at all.

When I got in to my "new home," there were some fresh flowers on my little white kitchen table which was just by the window facing Hermosa Beach Blvd. Shelly was all excited to show me everything in the house. The first night in my house, I called my dad to see how he was doing and to tell him the great news. I explained everything about my job, with Hawaii, my own studio apartment, etc. and said that everything had worked out so well for me. I believe my father could hear the excitement in my voice even though he was drunk. Still I could hear in his voice how happy he was for me. My father also sounded relieved now when he heard I got a job, house and had found a way to earn money. Our relationship had changed since we had that wonderful talk New Year's Eve. It just hurt me to hear how sad and miserable my father was. It made me upset with Liza for taking their sons, my brothers, from Spain to Sweden without even letting dad know.

I was going to work Tuesday through Saturday and I will have Sunday and Monday off. I would start 7:30 a.m. every morning and work until Sue didn't need me more that day. I would also work every Saturday night as Sue and her husband had a set date every Saturday. Usually, Sue said, they don't stay out so late and it would leave time for me to go out and meet with my friends if I wanted to later on Saturday nights.

My days were mostly busy and I didn't have a chance to think too much, but at night when I got to my house and was all by myself, that was when I start to feel alone and frightened. I did not sleep well at night, the nightmares kept waking me up. Still I had the energy I needed to deal with the kids and my other work duties during the day. Although I tried, it wasn't easy to stop myself from thinking about my past, I just could not erase it from my mind.

January 23, 2000 Golden Globes at The Beverly Hilton and Danny had three passes for Rita so she invited Sue and me to go with her. We all dressed up and I was so excited to see all the famous people on the red carpet. We had access to a room, where we drank champagne, and had a great time. It was kind of difficult to see from where we were, so Rita turned on the TV and all three of us jumped in the bed. We ate snacks and ordered up some more champagne while we watched 2000 Golden Globes on TV while it was going on downstairs at the hotel. My best friend, my boss and I hanging out together! I haven't felt this happy in a long, long time. I spent the night in Rita's house, and as always, I slept like a baby when I was there.

Actually, in Rita's house is the only time when I get some real good sleep.

One day off and back to work but I didn't mind because I already felt like a family member at the Sandersens. In the morning when I came down, Sue and Rob were there and Rob came over to give me a hug, as if it was the most natural thing in the world. I could feel in my heart that this is exactly what I needed. When the kids were at school and the errands were done, Sue and I had lunch together. All we talked about was the Golden Globes, and how much fun we had.

Sue sent me to pick up Rob at school by myself for the very first time and it felt so nice to get that responsibility, to do things by myself. When Rob saw me, he ran towards me with his arms outstretched for a hug. The days passed and just when I thought everything finally was falling into place, something happened that put me in a position where I had to make a very painful decision.

January 27 at 7:30 a.m. when I came down to the kitchen to feed the kids and make sure they got to school on time, my cell phone rang. It was my sister calling me from Sweden and the first thing Annie asked me was

"Hey sister, what are you doing?"

"I just got to work to start my day."

"Is someone there or are you alone?"

Now I really start to get a creepy feeling and said, "I am not alone. Sue and the kids are here."

"Can you sit down; I have something to tell you?"

Without sitting down I said, "What's going on Annie?"

"Liza just called me an hour ago Hannah and our dad died this morning."

"What?"

I thought I was going to faint when Sue came over, grabbed my arm and put me on a chair. "Hannah was going on, did something happen?"

By now, all the color had drained from my face. I looked up at Sue, my mind was whirling and I could not believe what my sister just told me. My dad, my father is dead…gone? I spoke to him a week ago and I will never talk to him again?

"Annie, let me call you back."

"Ok I know you're working but I wanted you to know."

"Hey sis, it is ok, thank you for letting me know."

We hang up and my tears start to fall down my cheek while Sue looked at me and said "No good news huh?"

"No, it was my sister and she just told me our father died today, this morning."

"Oh my God Hannah," Sue said and came over and took me in her arms, rocked me slowly back and forth.

Sue started to cry as well. Shelly who just came into the kitchen got upset when she saw that both her mother and me crying. Sue stroked my hair and told me to take some time off and that she would take care of her kids today, and if I wanted, she would take me to Rita and Danny's as soon as Shelly and Rob were settled in school. It was with sad eyes both of the children gave me a firm hug and I could still feel the touch from their little arms comforting me as I saw them leave in the car to go to school.

I walked around, like in a trance, back up the wooden stairs to my studio and I couldn't believe it. My father was just 51 years old and that's still so young, too young to be gone. I know my dad wasn't thinking about his diet even though he had diabetes, and in addition my father was an alcoholic. But still I think what really killed him was his unhappiness. I have the belief that no money in the world can buy happiness, and now for me my father was the proof. Honestly, I believe my dad stopped living a long time ago. I was anxious and I didn't want to be by myself today. I called Rita to see if I could go over there because I needed the comfort I find at her and Danny now. Rita was still at work but if I could find a way to get up there she said, Danny could come and pick me up after he was done working and take me to their house. I can't be alone now.

Sue dropped me at the hotel in Beverly Hills where Rita works and everyone at Rita's office express their condolences at my loss. Rita and I went out to lunch and I felt like I was in a coma. It was strange, because I didn't cry, but thought that the tears would probably come when the shock of it all was subsiding. Rita had to work after lunch and sat me down in the hotel restaurant to wait for Danny to come and pick me up. I asked for paper and a pen because I knew I would get the desire to write, especially now when all these feelings rushed over me. As soon as I picked up the pen to start, my tears filled my eyes and ran down my cheeks and dripped on the empty paper. *Just when my father and I really started to understand and listen to each other. This would have been a new beginning for us.'* But even with the knowledge that my father was now in a better place and that he finally had peace of mind, I missed him so much. Danny came and he was holding and comforting me while he repeatedly whispered, "I am so sorry Hannah."

Danny took me to their house and I lay down in Rita's bed with the cats. I was so emotionally exhausted. Memories with my dad came over me and I remembered when I was 8 years old. My dad had just come home from Los Angeles after one of his business trips, and he brought home a deep blue shiny jacket for me. It was made of silk with HOLLYWOOD written in glitter on the back. I loved it and told my dad

"Daddy can you please take me with you next time you go to Los Angeles?"

"One day Hannah we can go on vacation, but I can't take you with me when I have to do business there. "

I was happy with that answer at that time. When I was nine years old and my sister and I had watched a thriller movie, I couldn't sleep for three nights, when I told my dad he again promised me,

"Hannah it is just a movie, not reality. When we are going to Los Angeles, we are going to a movie studio so you get a chance to see how they make movies. With that knowledge, you won't be frightened next time you see thriller movies again."

Once again, I thought it would happen one day but it was just another empty promise. The first time I actually put my foot in the United States, was when I came here by myself. Danny knocked at the door and opened it to see if I was awake.

"Hannah, I think we should open the champagne your boss gave me to celebrate your dad's life."

I got up and Danny opened the bottle, gave me a glass and said "What's your father's name and how do you say cheers in Swedish?"

"My father's name is….. I mean was," I corrected myself, "Eric Bonde and cheers in Swedish is skål."

"Skål, for the life of your father, Mr. Eric Bonde," Danny said, raised his glass and so did I.

"Skål pappa, I love you."

The phone rang and it was Sue. She just wanted to hear how I was doing. Rob and Shelly had been worried about me all day after they had seen me so sad earlier that morning. The whole family wanted to let me know they were there for me, if and whenever I need them.

Hearing that from Sue warmed my heart so very much. Even with this disaster it hit me how blessed I was to have such good friends and a great job. Before Danny went to bed that night, he took my hand and gave me a kiss on my forehead saying,

"Hannah you are a very strong woman and you will make it over here in California. Or wherever you decide to live, so please don't worry."

I tried to get some sleep but I was too upset to get any rest the whole night.

The following morning, before Rita and Danny had to go to work, I gave them both a hug and thanked them very much for all their support and for letting me come over. "Anytime Hannah. Our home is your home." And I know they meant every word.

I met Sue by Radio Shack and when we got back home we sat in the kitchen and talked over a cup of coffee, Sue said,

"You need to get your ticket now back to Sweden so you will have a chance to get there on time for the funeral."

That hadn't even crossed my mind as I knew I could not go. *'What am I going to tell her?'* I felt very scattered and right then, my mind was my worst enemy. *'What if I tell the truth, then she might think that I am crazy, and believe Shelly and Rob are in danger to be under my supervision and won't want me to work for them anymore. But if I lie…no I can't lie.'* I had promised myself that my new life would be built on the truth and only the truth. *'If she decides to fire me when I tell her about my crazy ex who wants to kill me, than I have to deal with it.'* I took a deep breath and said,

"No, I can't go."

"Of course you can Hannah," Sue said with a smile. "I want you to know that when you come back, we will still be here waiting for you."

45

I starred right in front of me, the big white stove and wooden drawers, the kitchen table with the couch on one side and two chairs on the other.

"I can't go Sue." Now I looked her in the eyes and I felt more comfortable as I continued, "If I go, I might not be able to come back. Someone in Sweden wants to kill me."

"WHAT? WHO wants to kill you?"

I hesitated again but reminded myself that it is not my fault that he is crazy. I'm not the one who needs to be ashamed.
"My ex boyfriend. I had to escape and run away from Sweden to save my life. That is how I ended up here in Los Angeles."

Sue looked around to see where the kids were. Rob sat on the stair playing his Game Boy. His dark hair was all messed up from the night and his brown eyes were still sleepy. He looked so innocent and cute. We couldn't see Shelly anywhere, so she was probably still asleep.

"Tell me about yourself Hannah." Sue turned toward me again. The tile was cold under my bare feet.

"You see, I met my crazy ex when I was fifteen, and he was seventeen. We had just been together for about two months the first time he hit me. I ended up spending almost fifteen years with him. Fifteen years where he had complete control over me and what I did. He abused me a few times per week. When I broke my ankle last summer, I realized he haven't changed at all. I had. So, my choice was either I marry him as we planned for the coming May and live my life like this, where I can't do or say what's on my mind without being beaten up, or I leave him. But I knew leaving him wouldn't be an easy option. I would have to leave my country and my family too. The only way he would let me get out of the relationship would be if I were dead."

Sue took both of my hands. I must have been freezing because the touch from her hands warmed my whole body.

"I left him and stayed at a Women's Shelter at first, but he found me there. The police sent me to another Women's Shelter. I spoke to him on the phone and as we spoke, he told me that he just needed to see me one more time. That's it. I knew what that meant. It would just take one time to kill me. A week later, I was on my way over here." Now I had a tired smile on my face. "That's why I can't go Sue."

I was waiting for her to react. Maybe tell me that I had to leave. Maybe Sue would think it was too dangerous to have me taking care of her kids, but instead she said,

"Hannah. You are doing the right thing. I know your father would rather see you here, alive, than to go back and risk your life. You can't get your father back anyway. You are safe here with us."

We hear little footsteps on the stairs coming down. It was the kids.

"Shell, give me back my Game boy" Rob yelled. Shelly came flying into the kitchen and grabbed her mother's skirt, "Mom, save me. Rob is mad at me."

"He wouldn't be mad at you if you stopped teasing him. Give back Rob his Game Boy."

Sue's eyes met mine and we both had a good laugh. Outside the ocean waves cracked on the beach, and the sun reflected on the deck. The bright white tile blinded me for a minute. A feeling of peace and that I belonged somewhere spread over and through my body. It was amazing how I, after only three weeks, could feel so connected to this family. Maybe it was because I never had a real family myself. I knew Sue was right but it hurt that I would never get the chance to say goodbye to my father. Not even at the funeral.

Now when I think about the talk we had on New Year's Eve, it feels like my father somehow said all that to close our bonds. When I had only a couple of weeks earlier had told him about my job, and that everything was going to be okay with me. I guess my dad could get peace of mind and let go. My father knew I'm strong and that I would be fine now that my situation had improved even though I didn't have my papers as yet. Dad knew I would make everything work for me. How my father knew? Because I was just like him, only stronger.

I had a hard time sleeping because it felt like my body was twitchy and uneasy. I was thinking a lot of my dad and that I couldn't go to his funeral. I was also thinking about my little brothers who will never get the chance to get to know our dad like I had. My father was going to be buried in Gothenburg, at the same cemetery as my grandparents.

Friday February 11th 2000 was my 30th birthday. Sue was planning to take the kids to Arizona to visit her friends over the weekend. When Stephan took them to the airport in the afternoon, he dropped me, a big birthday cake and a bottle of champagne the Sandersens had bought for me, at Rita's and Danny's house where I would spend the weekend.

Rita wasn't home yet and Danny was asleep in his room, but I had my own key and went in. I made myself a cup of coffee, sat down on the grey couch and turned on the TV. I felt like I was home visiting my family, so when their phone rang, I picked it up and with a cheerful voice answered,

"Hello."

"Hey Hannah, happy birthday." I heard someone saying in Swedish with a voice I recognized too well. It was Jared! *'I knew it. My life now was too good to be true, too good to last. My past is catching up to me.'* I closed my eyes and thought I was going to die. The question was *'how the hell did Jared get this number?'*

It felt like my whole world started to spin and that my past had a grip on me again. I just hung up the phone. I was now crying hard. I felt so helpless. All I wanted was to have a nice quiet life. But it seems like it's not going to happen. Not as long as Jared is alive. When Danny woke up and saw I'd been crying he asked,

"Hannah what is going on? You're supposed to be happy, it's your birthday."

"Jared just called me on your phone and wished me happy birthday. I don't know how to get rid of him. He was right, there is no way I can hide from him. I am so sorry Danny."

Danny came over and made me look at him by taking me under my chin and raised my head. "It's okay Hannah. He won't find you."

I apologized that Jared had gotten their number, although I had not given it to him. Same "old" bad habit that I feel guilty for what he is doing to other people. The last thing I want to do is to get my new friends involved in all this drama. I felt as helpless now as I did in the Women's Shelter when Jared found me. *What if Rita and Danny don't want to have anything to do with me now that Jared has their telephone number? It feels like I'm the one who has to suffer because of him even after I've left him. But how could I blame them if they made the decision not to have me around? It just makes me so sad to think that I could lose these two people I love and who are my friends because of him. Here I am, trying to build my own life and Jared is still able to mess it up. It just seems like it doesn't matter what I do, Jared will find me anyway.'* But I had promised myself one thing; I am going to live *my* life and there is nothing Jared can do to stop me.

I called my mother and asked if she was the one who had given Jared the telephone number? But, of course, my mom said no. It was a possibility that Liza gave the number to Jared as Liza thought that running away from my problem wouldn't help, and that there were other ways to work things out, and my situation 'hadn't been that bad.' That was easy for Liza to say because she did not know anything about what was going on with me through the years. Liza knew Jared was abusing me, but she wasn't aware of how serious it had been and she wasn't the one taking the abuse. My sister called Liza to ask her, but she of course denied it.

My mind was occupied with trying to figure out how Jared got the telephone number when I have no formal connection to the house or the telephone number in any way. Then it crossed my mind, and I know Jared is able to do it. Jared might have broken into my mother's apartment when my mom was out, gotten the number and left. She wouldn't even notice Jared had been there. My mother does not take notice of details as I do. She is more naive and if something has been moved around, she wouldn't even have noticed it.

I had already told her not to leave any information about me anywhere in the apartment. I had told her, when she leaves the apartment, so should my information but I guess my mother, once again, didn't pay attention to what I'd told her. Sometimes it makes me so frustrated when I tell my mother something important, and she ignores it and doesn't take it seriously. How could she not? She saw what Jared had done to me, and how battered and bruised I was when she met me at the hospital where they documented everything. But that's my mother! We are so different she and I. I do what I have to do but my mom has the mentality -- if she puts her head in the sand so she won't see it, the issue or problem might disappear.

So back to Jared -- people underestimate others so easily -- but I've been there done that! I lived with him for 15 years so I know how his mind works and what Jared is capable of. There is no way I would ever underestimate him. I would never think Jared can't get to me. If that day comes, I pray that I kill him before he kills me.

I called Rita at work and told her what had happened. I could hear in her voice that she wasn't pleased. Not happy at all about it. Once again, I apologized for him getting the telephone number and if she and Danny wanted me to leave them alone, I would understand.

"Let's talk about it when I get home Hannah, but don't worry about it now ok."

"Of course I worry about it. Everything that has to do with Jared and my past worries me."

Hawaii-time

My suitcase was opened on my bed and I looked at my clothes but it felt like my whole mind was empty. *What am I going to take with me and how is the weather there now? Is there anything for me to do on my days off? I wonder how it looks over there?*' It was my first trip to Hawaii and I was very excited, but I got flashbacks to when I was still in Sweden. The last time I packed my suitcase, or re-packed what Jared had put in my suitcase maybe is more correct to say, was when I left Sweden to come over here and now suddenly I remembered how kind of numb I was at the time. Now I knew at least what I am going to be doing in Hawaii and that I was not alone. In Kungalv at the Women's Shelter, I had no idea what was in store for me over here or what was going to happen when I got here.

I looked at the time and I had to hurry up to get the packing done. It would be time to leave soon. I packed the lightest clothes I had but even those would be too hot. I left Sweden in November, which means I just had winter clothes when I arrived here. I hadn't had a chance or money to buy some clothes that fit the Southern California weather, so I had to do the best with what I had. When I came down to the kitchen and Sue saw me, she laughed and said,

"Do you think we are going to the North Pole or something?"

"No, but I don't have any lighter clothes yet," I replied and smiled.

"No, I know. I was just kidding. There is a great store where you can get some nice clothes when we get to Kauai, and it is cheap too."

"That sounds pretty good to me."

Rita had told me that Hawaii is a beautiful place and I was lucky to have the chance to go there. Sue, Shelly, Rob and I would leave first and Stephan would come later. He still had some business to take care of here in Los Angeles. Stephan drove us to the airport and as soon as we got close to LAX, I got a strange feeling in my stomach. Almost as if I was about to panicking. *'Oh stop Hannah you are not going back to Sweden and you are not alone this time. Stop stressing so much,'* I told myself.

We checked in and even though I'd been a little worried to fly with the kids, I had both of the kids in couch class while Sue was in first class, there was no need to worry. Everything went very well, Rob and Shelly were more accustomed to fly than I was although they were young kids. We had a great time on the plane, but from time to time the kids were fighting over whose turn it was to sit in my lap. I had both Shelly and Rob close to me so I could see where they were at all times. I protected them as if they were my own. Even when we crossed streets or walked on the sidewalk, I always made sure I was closest to the cars, the danger. I had my body as a shield for them and remembered how unsafe I had felt as a child. I would never let anything happen to Shelly and Rob as long as I was there. Both of them trusted me and knew I would always be there whenever they needed me. Sue came over to see how everything was going for us and to bring me a glass of wine.

I was so lucky to have a boss like her. We had to change flights in Honolulu but we did not have any time to look around. We just get off one airplane and got onto the next one, which took us to Kauai. It was a smaller plane and we all sat together as there was no couch or first class. Rob and Shelly had been resting on the big plane and now they started to get excited. We arrived in Kauai and were waiting for our luggage and I had my hands full trying to keep the children calm.

"Can we just go home now? When is Nana coming to get us? How long do we have to wait?"

Finally Nana came with the van. She was a very nice woman from Kauai, who was the caretaker of Sandersen's property when the family was away. When Sandersens came, Nana helped out with whatever the family needed her to do. It was more housekeeping now that I was there to take care of the kids.

The first thing Sue, Nana and I did when we got to the house was to unpack the van. Later when we were done unpacking, Sue showed me the "pool cottage" which was going to be my house while we were there. On the property was also the "Japanese guesthouse" also called "The love shack", which they either rented out if they did not have friends visiting and there was of course, the main house.

The main house, reminded me of the house where I grew up, the house my father built for our family in Landvetter. It was built mostly in wood, high ceilings and had an amazing view. The main house was closest to the cliff and all you saw when you looked out over the backyard, was the open light blue-green ocean and you could see the dolphins playing in the ocean. The beauty took my breath away. The Sandersens also had four horses and I couldn't wait to see them. After dinner, I asked if I could be excused and go to unpack my own stuff? I was so tired.

"Sure you can and we see you tomorrow morning around 9-9:30 a.m., okay."

"Okay."

Rob and Shelly gave me hugs and kisses before I said good night and left.

I came into "my house" and it was like a studio, with a kitchen and a bathroom. I unpacked the few things that I had, and then I went out on my little patio by my kitchen. I couldn't hear anything but the horses in the stable, which was located closest to my house. It felt so calm and peaceful. I knew this would be a great place to start my healing, just what I needed at this point in my life. Outside, it was so much darker than Los Angeles. LA has so many street lights everywhere. When I looked up, the sky was filled with stars. I hadn't noticed anything like that in a long time.

While I was standing there, my mind went back to Sweden and the life I've had there. I was thinking about times when Jared and I were supposed to have a nice time and just a word could change the best time to one of the worst times. It would be a time when I was beaten up, raped or forced to do things I didn't want to do. I was thinking about all the stress when I did my best to try manage our money and pay our bills, instead Jared took the money and invested it in his karate studio OGK or something else. We barely had food for the day and could not pay the rent.

Since I first met Jared, he had been talking about how to make money. Talk was all Jared did. He had "business" ideas and invested not just his own but my money as well. We lost everything and more. I told Jared that he could do whatever he wanted and invest the money we had left after our bills were paid, but no, he just told me to step back and shut my mouth as he could do whatever he wanted to do without asking me. If I said anything about "but it's my money too" Jared always replied, "Fatsos don't have any money. The paycheck you are getting is nothing and you owe me that money bitch, only for me putting up with your bullshit."

I shook my head to make those horrible memories go away, closed my eyes and prayed, *'Dear God. Forgive me for my mistakes and lead me the right way, to make the right decisions so I can build my life in this country. Thank you for bringing me to this family, for my family and especially for my friends here. A special thank you for my life and please help me to find all the strength that I need to be an independent strong woman.'* Now I got overwhelmed with emotion and my tears started to fall. I let them and continued *'and last, please keep everyone I know safe from Jared, Amen.'*

I went into my new home and got ready for bed. My first night in Hawaii and I felt lonelier then I did when I was in Hermosa. Now I was so far from my friends who had become somewhat my home, and being this far away, made me feel a little lost. I slept okay the first night but felt well rested when I got in the house the morning after. The kids were still asleep which made me surprised, but it gave me a chance to sit down and have a cup of coffee with Sue for once.

"So Shorty, how did you sleep last night?"
"I slept okay but last night some of my memories from Sweden came back."

"Were they good ones?"

"No, only some of the bad ones. Unfortunately I got more bad memories than good ones. Why can't I just forget about it now when I am here, on the other side of the world?"

"What you've been through in your life is trauma Hannah, you got to give yourself time, okay?"

"Sue it still hurts so much, and every night when I close my eyes I am scared that when I open them again, Jared will be there. I feel as if the freedom I have, my friends and you are too good to be true for me. It is like a dream I will wake up from soon and find myself back in the nightmare as a prisoner with him."

Sue comforted me, held me in her arms as she wiped my tears away.

"Hannah, you are safe now and especially here. You're even further from Sweden now than where you were in California. Jared would never look for you all the way over here."

"If Jared had any clue that I was here, he would. For Jared there is no distance too far to get the revenge he wants. Jared is the most evil person that ever has existed."

The days in Kauai were wonderful. We went to the beach or hung around by the pool most of the days and in the afternoons Rob had karate practice with his friends Larry and Shane, or they just had play dates. It was difficult for me in the beginning to take the kids to their karate practice. I got flashbacks regarding how disciplined one is supposed to be, and how different the reality could be. At least the reality with Jared.

On Kauai, I got off earlier than when we were in Los Angeles and those times I could feel the loneliness come creeping up on me. I was anxious and got very agitated, which made my mind become my worst enemy from time to time. I spent many hours talking on the phone, and there were times I couldn't reach any of my friends and left messages. I was almost panicky at times, thinking my friends didn't answer because they didn't want to deal with me and my drama anymore. All this fear because I'd been through so much bullshit and believed people must think I was a weak drama queen and just had issues. Of course that wasn't the case, but my self-esteem was very low after all those years of physically and mentally cruelty.

When I think of my past, the early years of my life, it hurts so very much – to not having someone I could depend on. Then another thought interrupted, those years when Jared and I had a relationship, the emotional rollercoaster, still not having someone I trusted enough to help me. That last week between my first attempt when I tried to leave him until I succeeded the second attempt, when Jared locked me in our apartment .... And that week Jared tortured me worse than ever and almost killed me when he realized that he had lost control over me. Those memories hurt so very much.

But I have come to realize that it was necessary for me to leave not only Jared, but my whole family, in order for me to get a life, my *own* life. Those thoughts made me feel ashamed and guilty in reference to my family. It wasn't that I didn't care for them or love them, but everyone in my family had dumped so much of their issues on me throughout my life, and I had tried to help them as much as I could, that I forgot to take care of the most important person, me. Since I moved to the US, I did what I should have done so very long ago, take care of and look after me. Make myself number one. I did not have the strength and I couldn't take care of my family any more, I now had to put myself first.

Even though Jared was so unbelievably cruel to me, I still didn't want anything bad to happen to him. I was still scared of him and if anything bad happen, Jared would blame me, as he always had. He worked hard to brainwash me and control me. The nightmares kept repeating, over and over and made me realize that Jared really had a hold on me. I have to keep reminding myself that Jared is in Sweden and I am safe here in the US. At least that is what everyone keeps telling me, but I knew better. I know I'm not safe anywhere and I will never be safe anywhere, until I am told that Jared is dead!

When we got back from Hawaii, things were getting back to normal, with the everyday routine here in Los Angeles and another month and a half before summer and three months back in Hawaii.

Hawaii time again

Packing was easier this time, because I knew what to expect and I had clothes more appropriate for the weather. The last time we went to Hawaii, I had bought clothes and now I couldn't wait to go back to Kauai. I actually missed Hawaii and the calm and relaxed tempo. It was getting easier to deal with my emotions from my past and to work on building my strength. I had to feel everything that came up for me, the pain, the fear, the hurt and the sorrow, in order to move up from the deep and try to move forward.

Back in Los Angeles with friends around, it was easy to get distracted, even though I knew I should allow myself to experience the different emotions, to be able to let go and heal. While in Hawaii, I did not have that distraction and I spent my free days alone.

I had already said goodbye to Chrystal and my other friends but I knew I would miss them. When we took off from LAX, it was as if all the stress I felt in my stomach earlier, I was leaving behind in Los Angeles and a kind of peace filled me. There would be no stress for three months, just calm, serene beauty and the freedom to think and heal some more.

Hawaii was nice as always and again as soon as I got there so many emotions came over me. I had so much hurt and had been through so much pain all my life. Back home in LA it was easier to "run away" from my feelings, but here I just had to face and feel them. It forced me to think of what I'd done. I had escaped my past to save my life! I could think of what I needed and wanted to do with my life from here forward. To move on, I needed to put my past behind me, but it wasn't so easy. I hadn't been aware of it before. What trauma I'd been through and how much damage had been done to me. I believe I did not want to see it or deal with it, as the pain was horribly indescribable.

Sometimes I thought I had successfully let it go, only to be awakened one night or another by a nightmare where I was imprisoned by Jared again, and close to a panic attack with shortness of breath. I was far from free from my past and the nightmares haunted me at least a few nights per week.

The days I spent with the kids went well, and they kept my mind occupied and focused. Both Shelly and Rob were easy going and now in the summer, they just enjoyed being on Kauai. The days looked almost the same, breakfast while watching TV, brushing out the tangles in Shelly's blond hair and trying to brush Rob's teeth while he was telling me everything on his mind. Patiently I managed to get it done somehow, and all those small details brought a smile to my face. Now the three of us were ready to get in the car and leave. First it was tennis camp for a few hours, and after that we stopped in the little village Kapa'a. We bought ice cream or shaved ice, which was what the kids preferred, from our favorite ice cream store and one day while the kids and I sat down on bench right outside the store talking Rob suddenly said, "My favorite ice cream is Hannah." Then he looked at me with his hazel brown eyes with the honesty of a child and before I had a chance to say anything, Rob continued, "Because I love you Hannah."

Close to tears from those loving and genuine words, my heart melted just like the ice cream in the sun. I stroked his dark brown hair and gave him a hug.

"Thank you sweetie. I love you too."

After the ice cream, we headed towards the karate studio where both Rob and Shelly practiced. When we got back home it was dinnertime. When that was taken care of, I had to make sure the kids took a shower or a bath. This same night when I had said good night and walked to my cottage, I started feeling anxious again. This seemed to happen when I know I will be alone but I pushed the thought away. It was quiet and empty in my cottage, not even a lizard as far as my eye could see, to talk to. I got paper and pen, wrote a bit in my journal before I took a shower, just to relax for the evening before I sat down in front of the TV and watched the series "Friends".

I used to watch that show in Sweden also, always dreaming and wishing that I'd had friends like that. Now I had found real friends, like Chrystal, Rita and Danny. I started to get that lonesome, needy feeling inside me again and thought *'it is because I do not have anyone to talk to. I better go to bed. Tomorrow everything will feel better.'* I turned off the light, got in bed and closed my eyes. I wish I'd had someone holding me. A nice loving man who was there to tell me everything would be okay. *Stop dreaming Hannah and go to sleep,* I told myself and after some tossing and turning, I finally fell into a restless sleep. I had all the time in the world to listen to my mind chatter while I was here on the garden island, and as a result, I realized why I was restless at night. I missed my mom.

I talked to Sue and asked if my mom came to visit me, if I could get some time off and could mom stay with me. Sue thought it was a great idea and we would work it out so I could get some time off. I had, after all, two weeks paid vacation saved up, Sue told me. I know my mom would say there is no money, but I was going to surprise her and buy the ticket for her birthday. I must see her and spend some time with her.

I called my mother and asked if she would come if I bought the ticket for her birthday, and she said yes. I arranged everything and purchased the ticket and started the countdown to the date when I would see my mother again. We got back to LA from Hawaii. Rob and Shelly started school again and things went back to the normal routine. I was happier than before and could not wait for the day when my mom would arrive.

My mom's first visit

October 2, 2000 the first time my mother came to visit me. I hadn't seen her since I left Sweden eleven months ago. I had barely slept the night before, I was too excited. And all morning as I was out running errands I was trying my best to distract myself.

On my way to LAX, I stopped at Costco and bought my mother some yellow and red sunflowers. As I headed towards the airport, I felt that anxiousness in my stomach as I always did when I was around the airport. Now that feeling got stronger as I parked the car and went to the arrivals terminal to meet my mother. I walked back and forth, forth and back, and asked two people who worked there,

"Is this the only Terminal 2?"

They both smiled at me,

"Yes it is. Just relax, whoever it is you are waiting for will be here soon."

"Is it that obvious that I am nervous?"

"Yes it is."

"Great," I smiled. "Thank you."

When I turn towards where the arrivals are coming out, my mother was already there. I saw mom before she saw me and I walked toward her. When she saw me, she dropped her suitcase and we embraced while her tears were falling and so did my. The existing passengers had to walk around us. When we were somewhat composed, I picked up mom's suitcase and said, "Let's go home mom, before they kick us out." Both mom and I laughed out loud.

On our way back to the house, I drove along the beach and pointed out different spots as we went by. I also pointed out the way to Rita's and Danny's, where I stayed when I first arrived here in the US. I really enjoyed being reunited with my mother. I knew this was going to be a wonderful couple of weeks. I parked the car and went into the kitchen to drop off the car keys and the papers I had for Sue. Sue hugged mom and asked if she had a good trip. I was pleased to see how the Sandersens welcomed mom. I introduced mom to Rob, he looked at her with a quizzical look on his face, and then he looked at me.

"Who is she Hannah?"

"She's my mom Rob", I said and ruffled his hair with my fingers.

"Oh." That was all Rob said and went back to play with Ted, one of his best friends. I thought to myself, *'why is Rob acting so strange?'* Then Shelly came running into the den where we were and hugged my mother so I introduced her also.

Mom and I finally got up to my house and while mom unpacked we talked nonstop.

Rob kept acting strangely, being somewhat rudely. I had to ask Sue to talk with him to find out what was wrong. Sue found out that through a child's eye and in Rob's mind, he said he did not like my mother. He thought she was here to take me away, to take me back home. Sue and I had to explain to Rob that my mother was only here to visit me, and that the US is now my home. After the explanation, Rob was back to the handsome charmer that he is.

While my mother was here, I had ten well-deserved days off. I had just bought my own car. Mom and I visited many sights, went to Beverly Hills, Santa Monica, Hollywood and a one-day trip to Disneyland.

I made sure mom had a chance to meet my friends, Chrystal, Rita and Danny. She brought gift for Rita and Danny, a "thank you" to let them know how much she appreciated everything they both did for me, their exceptional kindness. I also took mom to the Swedish church in San Pedro to meet Anna and Mike, and to show her around as I related the story of how I had survived since I arrived. The two weeks of my mother's visit just flew by and when it was time for my mother to leave, it was with heavy heart and lots of emotions I took her to the airport for another "good-bye".

We hugged and the tears started. After we said goodbye and then watched my mother clear Customs, I walked to the car with sadness in my heart. I did not care that my mascara left black traces on my cheeks and that everybody could see I was crying. I missed my mother already and only God knew when or if I would have a chance to see her again.

Well getting back to the present and having to carry on, I mentioned to Sue in the course of chatting about this and that, that I hadn't had my period since I was seventeen. She told me that she knew a chiropractor that she suggests that I should see. He had worked on friends she knew and managed to get them back on track. It was easy to convince me to make an appointment with Dr. Lou. Once there, the nurse took blood tests and when the results arrived a few weeks later, Dr. Lou had the answer; my thyroid level was very low. I had hypothyroidism, he said.

Dr. Lou told me that I needed to take medication for the rest of my life. Low thyroid causes many issues like difficulty with weight loss, coldness, tiredness etc. I started taking medication the same day, and a few months later my period began for the first time in thirteen years. I was so happy to have my period even though it still wasn't regular. I menstruated every third month, or so, then every two months and now I have my period every month. I finally understood that it all goes in a circle, no stress, normal thyroids and regular workouts, all help me to have a normal life. I noticed when I am extremely stressed, my menses is always late.

My first Halloween

Chrystal and I had talked about what to do on my first Halloween in the US. Swedes do not celebrate Halloween as it is done here, so I was excited. After we talked back and forth, we decided to dress up as ABBA and go to The Kingshead and sing karaoke. That was the perfect choice. Abba was a Swedish group with two women and two men. But there was a problem; we did not have any men to complete our ABBA group. So Chrystal came up with the brilliant idea to create our own guys. We took stockings and packed them with newspaper to make arms and legs. For heads, we used wigs stands, painted on faces and put wigs on them. There they were, Benny and Björn!

Chrystal would be the blond Agnetha and I would be the hot red head Anni Frid. We both wore long hair wigs, Chrystal wore pink pants and I wore a black skirt and all four of us had white T-shirts. Chrystal and I had an A on our T-shirts and the guys had a B on theirs. On our way down the street to The Kingshead, Chrystal and I on the end with the guys between us, our T-shirts spelled ABBA. There was no mistaking who we were supposed to be. Nicolas the security guy just smiled at us when he saw us.

At The Kingshead, everyone loved our costumes including our guys. Chrystal and I performed an ABBA song, Waterloo, with the dance we practiced to complete our costume. Dray and Patrick who were in charge of the karaoke, held "our" guys and pretended they were dancing and singing along with us. We had a blast! I felt like a kid again. It had been many years since I had this much fun and enjoyed it. Happy and exhausted after the evening, I fell asleep with a smile on my face as soon as I got home and got into bed.

Hawaii 3rd time

It was early in the morning when Sue called and woke me up. I got in the shower and as I let the hot water stream over my body, I felt some resentment because I wasn't ready to leave for Hawaii again, not just then. However, I did not have a choice.

As we arrived to Kauai, our luggage was already there so we packed everything in the van and headed home. We all were tired and that same evening, Sue and I got upset with each other. She said something, and her tone it was almost as if she owned me. *'No one owns me, and no money in the world can buy me,'* I thought.

The following morning after I got back from my walk, there was a note on my door from Sue. I got that knowing defensive feeling in my body. I took a shower and thought about my job situation and why I felt such resentment to leave LA this time. I guess I had grown out of the position and had done all I could for this family. Now that I had a foundation here with my finances under control, and had my own car and started to network, it was time for a change.

New job January 2001

I realized it was time for me to take my life to another level and continue to build and move forward in life. I had some kind of stabilization, but to be a live-in nanny as I was, was limiting me with the planning of my personal time. I wanted to join a gym and have my own schedule as to when to go, but with my work schedule, I never knew what time I would be getting off work. It could be 5:00 p.m., or it could be midnight. I never knew what time in advance and if I made plans for a gym class, I might have to cancel. I just wanted some more structure in my life. I also started to miss my friends too much when we were in Hawaii. I felt lonelier there each time we travelled. I was also tired of working on Saturdays. My whole life I'd had jobs where I had to work weekends and holidays. It was time to get a job with "office" hours.

I had been telling Chrystal how I felt and she was missing me too when I wasn't in LA. She was going through some difficulty in her life also. She had decided to divorce her husband Christopher, but she and Aaron were going to stay in the house and Christopher would move out. Chrystal could use some help with money and suggested I could rent a room in her house. I jumped at the suggestion right away. It would be so much fun as Chrystal and I were spending almost all my time off together anyway.

I looked for a new position but this time for a live-out position where I did not have to live where I worked. It took me a few days to get in the right frame of mind and get up the courage to tell Sue I wanted to talk to her. The whole family had come to mean so much to me and both kids really liked me, especially Rob.

"Sue I feel I can't give your family all the time you need from me anymore. You see, I think I want to separate my job and life, where it would feel more like a regular job, where I would have set hours to work. It's not that I don't like to work for you but…."

"Hannah I know exactly what you mean and we understand. It's time for you to move on, and even though Rob and Shelly will miss you and be sad about it, they will eventually understand.

And, after all you will still be in our life, honey. Just because you don't work for us doesn't mean we have to say goodbye."

I was so happy and relieved after our talk I hugged Sue.

"Thank you for understanding."

"Thank you Hannah, for being so wonderful to all of us. And for taking such good care of the most important thing in our life, our kids."

I gave Sue 30 days' notice so she would have time to find replacement help although I did not have another job as yet. I checked LA Times classified every day and I went to a nanny agency in the San Fernando Valley to see if they had any jobs of interest available for me to apply for. While waiting to see the owner, a girl came in and talked with the secretary. I heard and recognized her accent and asked her where she was from. She turns around while answering,

"I'm from Sweden."

I laughed out loud. "Me too." I said in Swedish and we introduced ourselves. Her name is Anja. We talked and talked until the secretary told me that the owner Rick was ready to see me. Anja and I exchanged phone numbers and we said goodbye. When I get home I couldn't wait to call Chrystal, I was so excited I had to tell her about Anja. But before the agency got back to me to offer me a position, I saw a LA Times advertisement about a job vacancy that caught my interest. I called and we arranged an interview and to meet the family at their house. They lived in Century City and had three kids, two girls and a boy. Chrystal met me and took me over to their house. She did not want me going alone to someone's house the first time.

The family was Jewish and lived in a condominium in a gated community right by Avenue of the Stars. They seemed to be a very warm, friendly and a nice family.

The youngest girl, Sarah, was three and half years old, her sister Limore was ten, and Ariyeh, their son, was fourteen.

The Fishers asked if I could cook and I told them I cooked a bit. Then Anat, the mother, asked if I knew how to cook Kosher. I didn't even know what that meant at the time. "I have no idea, but I learn very quickly," I hurried to add. Anat was going to check my references and call me back. Meanwhile, I was still looking for other positions. Sue told me when Anat had called her and I figured that was a good sign. It meant that Anat at least was interested in hiring me.

One day while Sue, her mother Ruby, and I were having a conversation the phone rang and by the way Sue reacted, I knew it had to be Anat. Sue put the call on hold and turned to me with a smile, "Hannah you have an offer on line 3" and she handed me the telephone.

"Hello."

"Hello Hannah, it's Anat. How are you?"

"I'm great. How are you guys doing?"

"Fine thanks. Hannah you have a lot of people around who love you, and we would love to have you in our family."

"Have you talked to your kids to see if they agree with you?"

It is important for me to know because it will be the kids who I would be working with most of the time. Anat laughed,

"All three of them have been doing nothing else but pestering me to call you before you found something else."

I was happy to hear that the Fishers had already gotten a good feeling about me when we met. They needed someone right away but decided that they would wait for me until I was available, and told me the position was mine if I wanted it. I said yes, of course, and that I would start in two weeks from Monday. I had a lot of things to do before then. I had better get started.

It was time to start packing my things and also to tell the kids that I would not be taking care of them anymore. Shelly took it really well while Rob became very upset. He locked himself in the bathroom, he was crying and refused to come out or let anyone in. It hurt to see Rob so sad. But when he finally opened the bathroom door and came out, I took the opportunity to explain to him why I was leaving.

"I'm not going to disappear from your life Rob. I'm just not going to be here every day, but I will still come to visit you. You will still see me." I stroked him over his head and Rob put his arms around my neck.

"I love you Hannah."

"I love you too Rob."

Sue found someone to fill the position and replace me and on February 5, 2001, I started my new job. I had rented a room at Chrystal's house and had moved in. A new job, a new home in a new area, but I felt I had made the right decision to move on with my life.

The Fishers and I got along very well. I understood and saw that the whole family was very close, a close-knit family. That was beautiful to see. I had always dreamed of having a large family, but that did not happen. I had observed and admired what it was like to have a *real* family at the Sandersens. Now my "new" family was the Fishers.

My experience and knowledge grew by working for a Jewish family, I learned about Jewish holidays, Bar/Bat Mitzvahs etc. Those times I went to the temple with the family for one reason or another, I really enjoyed listening to the rabbi speaking about the purpose of life and it was deep. Those words went straight in to my heart and soul. I learned how to cook Kosher and what Kosher means etc. I spent a lot of time with Sarah and we learnt different things from each other. If I couldn't find a word in English, I would explain it to Sarah and most of the time she knew the word.

I did my best to be fair to all three of children and taught them things the very best I knew how, and to give these kids what I never had as a child. We built up a trust between us. I told Ariyeh, Limore and Sarah to not hesitate to speak up and express their opinions. They had the freedom to say what was on their mind and they did not have to agree with what others said if they believed it was wrong, even if it was me. I wanted them to know that they could talk to me about anything. Limore and Sarah got in trouble at school on a couple occasions because they spoke up to the teachers. They told them that they didn't believe that was right and that they didn't agree with some statement or another. I smiled to know they had actually listened to me and became strong young girls who would speak up for themselves. I was and I still am, extremely proud of all three of them.

Even though I'd told my mother not to tell me if Jared had called, she always told me anyway. I came to a point where I actually called Jared up to see what he wanted, why he was stalking my family. That was not a smart move on my part because it meant that Jared still could manipulate me. At first, Jared just asked how I was doing and asked where I was. I told him that it was none of his business and that I can do whatever I wanted to do with my life. He said, the only reason he had contacted my family and wanted to talk to me, was to tell me that I don't need to run away from him. He had already forgiven me for leaving him. I was like, *'What?'*

And by the way, he continued, if he wants to find me it wouldn't be a problem. I got frustrated again and hung up the phone. *'Stupid me! Why did I even bother to call him?'*

The following day I called my mother and told her that if she tells me again just *one more time* that Jared called that I will have to change my telephone number and I won't give the new number to her. I didn't hear anything more for a while, other than in my nightmares. But it seems that Jared kept track of what my mother was doing, when she's home and if she's been out traveling. Jared was just trying to let me understand that he hasn't forgotten me. He thought he could still control me. If there is one thing I am sure of, it is that is not going to happen. Never again!

Met other Swedish girls

Anja and I stayed in touch although she lived in with the employer in Sherman Oaks. Chrystal and I invited Anja over to our home for an evening and she brought along another Swedish girl, Patricia. The four of us had dinner and it turned out to be a great visit with us talking and laughing and reminiscing about Sweden, one thing after another. We got along very well. When it was time for Anja and Patricia to leave, we had already set a date to go out partying together.

Patricia and Anja were about ten years younger than me, but who cared? It did'nt matter. Both Chrystal and I were happy to add new friends to our circle, so that night was the beginning of a great friendship for our Swedish girl group.

It was a Saturday and Chrystal and I decided to go out after we dropped Aaron at his dad's. We drove up to The Beverly Hilton valet parking to let Danny take care of her car and send us down to the club in the limo. The limo driver, Brosio, pulled up to the entrance to the club, got out and opened the door for us and hugged us then he left. I felt like a celebrity because everyone in line was looking at us like "who are these girls?"

More so when we passed the line and the bouncer let us in right away. We settled in and order drinks from the female bartender and she seemed quite friendly. She looked Scandinavian, blond and blue eyed, approximately 5-10 and slender.

I went to get another drink and asked the bartender where she was from. Her name was Catia and she was Swedish also. We spent a lot of time at the bar that night, talking to our new friend and eventually exchanged phone numbers so we could stay in touch. After the club, we just walked up to the hotel and got the car and drove home.

Two weeks later we did the same thing but this time it was four of us because Patricia and Anja came with us. We had a blast and were rocking on the dance floor all night. Patricia was getting into the freaky dancing and I was admiring her for how relaxed she was and didn't care who was looking at her. Although I have always loved to dance, I was somewhat stiff or stuffy to let go of my "can't do that" mentality, plus I was scared to even let a guy come close to me.

Chrystal and I kept in touch with Catia and she visited with us a couple of times. Catia told us that there was a Vegas trip planned for Memorial Day weekend with a couple of friends. She asked if we would like to go with them. I had never been to Las Vegas and I wanted to go. I had heard so much about it.

It was May 12, 2001, Patricia and I wanted to go out so I suggested going to the Shangrila in Hermosa Beach. I missed that place and even Bennie too. I was introduced to Bennie by Sue, he was her personal trainer and bartended at Shangrila. Patricia didn't have any other suggestions so off we went to Shangrila and we got there by 10 o'clock. When we arrived one of the security guard's pointed at me and said,

"Bennie's friend, right?"

"Yeah."

"Come this way,"

And he let us in right away ahead of the line. We had a great time and were talking to Bennie while we had our first drink and mingled; when we got our second one, it was time to get on the dance floor and almost right away a Black guy came over and asked if we wanted to dance. His name was Antione and both Patricia and I started dancing with him. Then Patricia left shortly after that. Unexpectedly, this guy sneaked up behind me on the dance floor and I don't know what happened, if it was the way he was dancing, or the way he was holding my waist, but he made me relaxed. I let go of all my fears or inhibitions and I was dancing as I never had before. Our bodies moved together like the perfect fit, like they hadn't done anything else. We together danced all night until the club turned up the lights at closing time.

"Hey Hannah, can I have your phone number? Maybe we can meet for coffee," he said and winked at me.

"Sure"

I wrote it down on a piece of paper and gave it to him. He continued,

"Thanks. You have to find your friend huh?"

"Yeah I do."

He gave me a hug and whispered in my ear, "I'll call you." I found Patricia and we left to drive back to the Valley where Patricia dropped me off at the house before she went home.

The following day Patricia and I had plans to go to The Beverly Center. We would drop the car at The Beverly Hilton and the limo would take us there. Catia called and I asked her if she wanted to come with us. She said she'd love to, so Patricia came for me first and we went over the hill to the west side and picked up Catia in Brentwood. From there we drove to Beverly Hills. Brosio, was happy to see us and he toured us around in the limo while we drank wine in the back seat and talked and laughed and had a good time. By the time we got to The Beverly Center we had finished a bottle of wine and had the giggles. We had an excellent time and when I went to bed that night, it was with a smile on my face. I was so happy to have friends like this and the freedom to enjoy life the way I like to enjoy it, and think I should enjoy it!

Monday, another week and it for work again. The day was kind of slow and I've had a long weekend so it was going to be early to bed tonight. Around 9:00 pm my cell phone rang and when I answered, it was Antione. I was happy to hear from him and we talked for about an hour. All the regular questions were asked and Antione didn't have any girlfriends or wife; he was 25 years old, he had his own company as he was studying as well. We talked about everything and Antione told me

71

he was going to Las Vegas as well Memorial Day weekend. Maybe we could hook up there?

Memorial weekend came up and Chrystal and I got in the car and headed for Las Vegas. The traffic was horrible, bumper-to-bumper. We finally arrived and after we were done with the check in, we went straight for the pool to hang out before the "happy hour". It was time to get ready for the night out so we all went to our rooms. Chrystal and I were ready to go and meet up with the others. I already knew Catia and the others had been doing drugs which I didn't like and had no part in at all. Plus the girls were competing with each other, who was the sexiest or prettiest, and I felt like an outsider. I do not care for competing with my friends, as I thought all that matters is that we are friends. Anyhow, once out on the strip, I needed to use the rest room, Catia and another girl also came along, but they used the bathroom to snort cocaine. That turned me completely off and killed the whole experience for me.

Suddenly I didn't like Las Vegas at all and I just wanted to go back to Los Angeles. As the evening passed by everything that could go wrong, went wrong. I missed Antione's calls and then we played phone tag for a while before we finally got a hold of each other. Antione asked if I want to hook up, which I was happy to do, but I had a hard time finding the place we were to meet and when I eventually got there, he wasn't there. I thought I'd missed him and sat down on a bench, frustrated and exhausted. *'It can't be worse than this.'* I looked through my phone book in my phone, trying to find Antione's number when I suddenly felt someone watching me. I looked up and Antione was standing a few steps from me, just looking at me. He smiled when he saw I'd seen him. I got up and walked over to him, put my arms around him and hid my face in his chest.

Antione took my hand and we start walking on Las Vegas strip hand in hand. I don't know what I would have done without him that weekend. Early in the morning, Antione dropped me off at the hotel and walked me up to the room. When it was time for Antione to leave, I took his hand between mine,

"Thank you so much Antione. You saved my trip."

He kissed me on the forehead,

"Anytime lil mama."

When I was lying in the bed, I thought about last night and a bad evening had turned into a great night. *'I don't want to like someone who's not ready for a relationship.'* But there was just one thing, I liked him already.

Back home and back to my normal routine and a few weeks later, June 2, 2001 came the next hit. It was a Saturday and I really wanted to go down to Shangrila again and asked Patricia if she want to go. She agreed and thought it would be fun. I talked to Sue about visiting with them at the same time and, of course, she told me we could stop by anytime. We spent an hour together at Sue's and then it was time for Sue and her mother to go out to dinner and so we left then as well.

As soon as we got to Shangrila, Bennie gave us a drink "on the house" after I had introduced Patricia to him and Anthony. We had two more drinks and danced when all of a sudden, I felt like I was about to pass out and couldn't remember what happened. My feet started to hurt. I took my shoes off and then Security kicked us out. I remember Patricia talking on my cell phone and then I lost her. Patricia was nowhere to be found.

I got to my car to wait for her but Patricia didn't show up. I asked a man who was walking by if he had a phone I could borrow to call Patricia on my phone. The man said he had one but it was in his car, it was a van parked just a few spots away, he would be happy to let me use his cell phone.

We got to the van and he opened the door. Suddenly I realized I had made a huge mistake, I had gotten in the car and he closed the doors. He got in on the driver side and then he locked the doors, and started the van. At that moment, I fumbled with lock on the door, trying to unlock it when the man tried to grab my hand. I finally got the door to open and slide down from the seat, jumped out and tried to run; it was more stumbling over to my own car. The man was so creepy and as soon as I got into my car, I locked the doors. He kept walking around the parking lot near where I was parked, so I started my car and left.

I was drunk and didn't even remember which way I took. Next thing I remembered, when I was driving on Sepulveda in El Segundo and I looked in the rear mirror, there is a police car behind me with the lights on…I was getting pulled over. In a second, my mind cleared up and I pulled to the curb. I was still barefoot and when the police officer came to my car, I smiled and said,

"Hey officer, how can I help you?"

"Can I see your driver license and registration please."

"Sure, here they are."

I handed the papers over to him and at that time, two other police officers had stopped as well and asked me to step out from the car. One of the officers asked if I had been drinking anything and I said I'd had one drink earlier in the evening but that was it. I was focusing as much as I could to talk clearly and the police officers put me through three sobriety tests. I failed all of them. The three officers looked at each other and one of them, Officer Smith, wanted to let me go, while the two others shook their heads.

"Can you please turn around and put your left arm on your back."

As I did, one of the officers took my wrist and put the handcuffs on me.

At that moment, my tears started to fall down my cheeks, I was sure the police would send me back to Sweden now. Back to the hell I escaped from. I knew this had been too good to be true and I didn't deserve to be this happy, to enjoy my life the way I'd done since I arrived here in the US. It has just been a taste of how great it feels to have a life and now it's time to send me back to hell, all because I fucked it up myself. While we drove to the station, Officer Smith asked if I was okay when he saw how devastated I was.

"No, sir, I'm not," and I just stared out the window. Officer Smith continued,

"Hey listen, you are not a bad person or a criminal. You didn't hurt anyone or yourself, so you'll be okay. You just need to sober up and then we will let you go home."

That was easy for the officer to say, when he don't know about my fears to be sent back to Sweden. I closed my eyes and the flashbacks came ... How Jared would tell me, "I told you Hannah, you can run but you can't hide, you can never get away from me," as he would laugh that sarcastic laugh he did when he was in control. I was so upset and so disappointed in myself. I would have the same stress as a hunted animal living in Sweden as long as Jared is there, all because I fucked it up.

I closed my eyes in the back of the police car as Officer Smith drove to the police station in El Segundo. *'How could I be this stupid?'* I thought and when I opened my eyes we were almost there. It was a female cop that was asking me all questions, a male police officer booked me, took my fingerprints, picture and filled out all paperwork.

The sobriety limit is 0.08 and I blew 0.17, more than double. So I was drunk! I was so cold and still barefoot and my body was shivering. One of the officers gave me a blanket and I sat down on the floor and let them finish everything up. Once in a while, someone asked me to sign papers and they could have given me anything to sign at that moment, I didn't care. I asked if I could make a phone call and the female police officer handed me the phone after dialing Chrystal for me.

"Where are you?" Chrystal said with an upset voice when she heard it was me.
"Patricia is on the way over here in a cab."
I felt even guiltier now when I heard how upset Chrystal was with me. I cried like a little girl and told her I was at the police station and what had happened. I was so happy to talk Swedish because in my condition, I barely could talk much less read English. While I was talking to her, my memory slowly start to come back and fill in some of the blank spaces. I got flash backs and remembered more things.

'After the creepy man tried to lock me in his van, I went back to Shangrila and asked the Security if I could come in because I needed to talk to Bennie. Robert, the main bouncer, told the other guy "don't let her in", so I asked if Robert could get Bennie for me, it was important, but he wouldn't even do that for me. The creepy man was circulating around keeping his eyes on me, and that was the time I got in my car and drove away.'

Chrystal got me back to reality by asking what had happened. I explained to her the best I could, and when Chrystal spoke again, her voice was calm. She told me to just take it easy and everything will be just fine. I had a very hard time to believe it would. This time I had really messed things up for myself. I was sure the police were going to send me back to Sweden, so how the hell is it going to be just fine?! My life was over!

"Hannah, let me talk to the police again and I'll make sure they don't put you together with anyone else. You just rest and as soon as they let you go, come straight home okay?"

"Okay."

I handed the phone back to the female officer and felt just like a kid who just had gotten instructions from a parent, but this was about how I just had blown my life. The male officer who had given me the blanket came out to me,

"Hannah come here. I'm going to take you to your cell for a few hours so you can get some sleep and sober up before we let you go home."

When he opened the door to where the cells and the other inmates were, I felt absolutely nothing. No fear, nothing. I was totally numb. He opened another door at the end of the corridor and there was another room with two cells but no one was in there, they were empty. He opened the door to one of the cells and handed me two blankets, "put this on you and try to get some sleep". He smiled at me but I didn't smile back. I just took the blankets, laid down on the bench, put one blanket under my head and the other on top of me and fell asleep right away. I was exhausted after all that had happened and just by thinking of all that was going to happen. The time must have been closer to 3:00 am if later.

I woke up as someone opened the door to the room and it was breakfast time. I'm not a big eater usually and today was impossible to even think of food. I just wanted to go home. I asked the officer who brought me breakfast,

"What time can I go?"

"Next time I come it will be time to let you go, how does that sound?"

"Great."

When she left, I lay down again and went back to sleep; it was the only way for me to remain calm. I was scared, real scared as my thoughts were running wild while I was awake. Along with the fear I felt guilty and I was my own worst enemy thinking about what I had done to myself. It was probably an hour or so later when the same officer came back in, opened the cell door and told me to follow her. They were about to release me and give me back my things, plus a paper with the date of August 2nd to appear in court. They also gave me a map showing how to get to my car.

When I got outside the station I looked at the map and tried to figure out how to get to my car, but that was easier said than done. I couldn't understand the map perhaps because I could not focus at all. I just wanted to get as far away as I could from the police. I grabbed my shoes in my hands and started walking while looking at the map, but I was lost. I walked over to a woman who had just parked her car ahead of me at the curb. I showed her the map and pointed to where the police said my car was parked and asked her if she knew how to get to that location. The woman tried to give me directions as she got out of her car. But, I guess seeing the frustration on my face the lady says,

"If you wait a minute while I go into the store to get me some water, I'll take you over there. It's a pretty far walk."

77

I couldn't believe the woman offered to take me there, and especially with my appearance having slept in my clothes. My eyes were red and bloodshot. The mascara was smudged under my eyes from crying. I was in party clothes from the night before, no shoes and dirty feet. I was a sight! The woman returned and opened her car door for me to get in and then she drove me around to look for my car. She found the area where my car was parked easily. I got out of her car and thanked her for helping finding my car. Before I drove off, I thanked God for keeping me safe and for the woman's help. We need more people like that in the world!

I still felt numb and thought I probably shouldn't be driving, but fortunately the traffic flowed easily and I got home very quickly. Patricia was asleep on a chair in the living room and looked up when I opened the door. She came over and put her arms around me as I started to cry. I whispered to her,

"I'm sorry."

"Shhh it's ok Hannah."

Chrystal also came and embraced me. Chrystal let me cry and held me until I calmed down before she took a step back and looked me up and down, from head to toe. "You look pretty darn good for having spent a night in jail girl," Chrystal said and we start laughing through the tears. Last night I wore a tight jeans tank top with fringes on the bottom and matching low cut jeans. We sat down and I showed them all the papers with my picture from the police "booking." Chrystal said, "Check out that picture! You look really hot and sexy with some naked skin, and your hair looks great."

Chrystal had to go to a birthday party with her son but before she left, Chrystal gave me a pill to calm my nerves, but I never took it. I do not like pills. Patricia had to go home and I was left alone. Again, guilt flushed over and through me and I was anxious and concerned. I ran a tub with water to help relax me while I left a somewhat broken message for Sue on her cell. I couldn't hold the tears back anymore. I crawled into bed and balled up like a fetus and fell asleep.

Sue's return call woke me up. She said she became worried when she heard my message. I told her the whole story of what happened. She told me to call Bennie and talk to him. What could Bennie do? The damage was already done and I'm going to have to pay for it. Only time will tell how much and in what way!

I called Bennie anyway and left a message and then I fell asleep again. The next time I woke up was when Bennie called. I told him what had happened and he said that if I would like, he would talk to Dean, who was another bartender at Shangrila. Dean was an attorney and would probably have some good advice on what I should do. I told him that I would really appreciate if he would talk to Dean.

When Chrystal and Aaron came home from the birthday party, I was awake. Chrystal made us tea and we talked about the situation. *How the hell could I be so stupid and drive when I had been drinking? What if I had an accident and killed myself, or even worse, hit or hurt an innocent passerby. I would never forgive myself. You're a looser Hannah. Yes, you wanted to get away from the creepy man, but to drive while drunk? There is no excuse, it's all on you Hannah.'*

Those thoughts made me feel worse and I felt absolutely worthless. I then started to wonder where did Patricia been when I couldn't reach her and when I got into trouble? *'I'll have to ask her when I see her next time.'* I was home all day and evening but I was walking around in a daze, like a zombie. That night my mother called me and I told her how much I had messed up. My mother got worried and I don't know if I had disappointed her, but it really didn't matter. What mattered was that I was disappointed in myself and I didn't know if I would ever be able to forgive myself for being so stupid.

When I went to bed, and my mind was retracing the events, I realized that I didn't know what papers I had signed at the police station. The officers could have given me my own execution papers to sign and I would have signed them. Or even worse, given me a gun to blow my head off. That's exactly how I felt and that my life was over anyway, so why wait and suffer. I was dejected, my eyes had lost their spark and I'd already given up on life it seemed. *'What the hell is going to happen with me? I'm the one telling people not to drink and drive, and to keep the faith at all times no matter what, and look at me now. Now I'm the one who had been driving drunk and lost all faith. I'll probably wake up soon. All this must be a nightmare.'* But the paper in my hand told me that I was going to court August 2nd, on my mother's birthday.

Patricia called the day after to see how I was doing and I told her the truth. I feel like shit. We decided to meet at Starbuck's for a coffee and talk about it, and thirty minutes later we sat face to face at Starbuck's.

"Patricia, where were you, and how come you didn't answer the phone when I called you?"

I had expected and maybe even would understand if her answer was anything but what it was. At that time when I tried to get a hold on her, and was almost kidnapped when I needed a phone. Patricia had my phone and I was lost and got pulled over by the police, Patricia was having sex on the beach with one of her booty calls from San Pedro. He is who Patricia was talking to when we got separated from each other. He drove up to Hermosa to meet her, and they were enjoying themselves, having sex on the beach. I had to be dealing with the bullshit I went through. I felt pressure in my chest and the anger within me woke up, but I told myself, *'I still cannot blame Patricia for any of what happened to me. I was still the one who fucked up and drove.'*

In the back of my mind, I knew it wouldn't be easy to not blame Patricia for some of my missteps. After all, friends are supposed to look out for each other and not let each other down.

Bennie called me back and said Dean, his attorney friend, wanted to talk to me. He gave me Dean's number and I called him. Dean was interested in handling my case so we arranged to meet and after I had told him everything, we both agreed to work together and he told me it was a simple case. I explained to him how worried I was about the possibility of deportation.

"It just can't happen Dean! I know I fucked up but I'd die if they deported me."

I am sure I sounded desperate and Dean could hear the dread behind my words. Dean looked at me and smiled,

"Don't worry Hannah. I will make sure you'll be safe. Most likely you don't even have to go to court."

Dean was able to represent me in court so I didn't have to show up. All during this time my emotions were as if I was on a roller coaster. Sometimes I was my "old" happy Hannah, and other times there was nothing that I could do to cheer me up or make me believe that everything would work out for me. One person I talked with and who helped me a lot to remain as calm, was Antione. I spoke to him almost every day, and Antione could hear the hopelessness in my voice every time, and he knew how terrified I was of my situation. Antione told me more than once,

"Hannah, be as nice to yourself as you are with others, and you'll be just fine."

I wasn't terrified for what would happen to me here, but how I would deal with my guilt, or what if they deport me. *How could I be this stupid? As if I was playing Russian roulette with my own life and it didn't matter if I lived or died, as long as Jared didn't get a hold of me. No wonder no one can love me.'*

Dean kept me updated of what was happening and he kept his promise that I didn't have to go to court. That was good enough he was there and represented me.

After a few months I got the judgment; It was 90 days restricted driver license, I was only allowed to drive to and from work, I had to pay a fine of $2000 and three months traffic school and six AA meetings. I was relieved, even though I would have to do all those things. As long as I did what the judge ordered and I didn't get into any more trouble, the court would be happy and wouldn't look any further into my background. They would not find out I was here illegally.

As soon as I learned what I needed to do, I signed up for traffic school, went to AA meetings and paid the fine. Months later, almost a year, I was finally done. I had done my duty and paid for my "crime". Now I had just the hardest part left to do, to forgive myself for making such a stupid mistake!

Girls Gone Wild

Mimi, Patricia and I hung out together most of the time; we could always find something to do together. Chrystal came with us from time to time when Aaron stayed with his dad. Every Saturday we went to one club or another either in the Valley, or Santa Monica, or Hollywood or somewhere else. Most Sundays we either went to the beach, out to dinner, or cooked dinner and just hung out together. We had a great time. We enjoyed each other's company so we started to go clubbing every Friday and Saturday, and even on Thursdays sometime. There were weeks when we went out five nights for the week. I was hyperactive, and always on the go so I had enough of energy for all of us as Mimi and Patricia kept telling me,

"There is no way we can keep up with you and expect, in ten years, to have as much energy as you."

I told them that I was just making up for all those years I had lost when I was in the relationship with Jared. Those years when I should have played around, hung out with friends, gone to college and done what teenagers usually do. Just living daily and not worrying about tomorrow. The things you need, as a young person, to get out of your system before you saddled down with just one person. To sow your wild oats! I had missed all of that, and had lived under strict control and fear of Jared. My complete youth had passed me by. Under my past and in Jared's control I had been messed up experiencing the wrong emotions of how life should be. I did not get to make my own decisions on what I wanted fearing what would happen to me if Jared did not approve. I was just now learning what I needed to do for myself and how get what I needed before I was ready for a relationship.

I did attract many favorable glances when the girls and I went out, but most of the men I met were younger than me, but no one cared. There were times I was interested in getting to know someone, or just interested in spending some time with him, but I lack confidence and I was somewhat hesitant to let anyone get close enough to really know me. I took many phone numbers but I always ending up erasing them, or I lost interest for one reason or another.

When you are young that is when you should spend the time experiencing and experimenting with life to prepare for adulthood. I had a lot of catching up to do and tried to do it all in a year and a half. It was intensive! There were a few times when I was intimate with a man, only because I felt lonely and wanted to be close to someone. The following day, I would feel guilty and beat myself up for using my body like that. But at least for the moment, I had someone holding me and I could pretend to feel safe and cared for. The guilt I would have to deal with later. I am definitely aware of how naive I was when I arrived to the US. But I was conscious of the games people played, the gamesmanship, and I didn't like that at all.

I thought it was better to give it to him right away before the emotions grew stronger, and if sex was the only thing he wanted, well, than it would not hurt as bad when he left me. Because I had no doubt that he was going to leave me, as everyone does, sooner or later, because my ex Jared told me so over and over. So I would give it up, just give the men what they wanted. My learned and practiced thought process was, if you don't give your partner what he wants, he will get it from someone else.

That did not seem to help me at all. I erased many phone numbers because either the other person did something dumb or there was no honesty to them that I could detect. If that wasn't it, I always found some reason, a reason to satisfy me that would end the relationship if there was the slightest chance for the relationship to become serious. Fear, I guess. By now I had learned I could not depend on anyone but myself. I guess some people thought I was weird, or maybe that was only in my own mind.

83

Beginning summer 2001 Patricia met Gary and they started dating. Gary took us Swedish girls to meet his friends and from time to time we would go out partying together. On the Fourth of July, Tom whom was a friend of Gary, invited some friends to his uncle's house for a BBQ and pool party. There was Tom and his girlfriend Laura, Tom's niece Jennie, Donald and his wife Mika and their little daughter Emily, Hunter and some other people. Tom has a large family so there were many people there. As soon as we got there, they made us feel very welcome and right at home. We had a wonderful time, and that was where Tom got the nickname "crazy" Tom. We Swedish girls named him 'crazy', but the people who knew him already had the same name for him.

Tom was flirting with all the girls, even though Laura, his girlfriend, was there. She smiled through the whole thing. In the beginning I couldn't understand how she could accept his behavior. But when I had spent more time with them, I understood that Tom would never cheat on his girlfriend. He was just a fun guy and his flirting wasn't serious. He was just playing around with words and Laura knew it. She trusted Tom and was confident that Tom loved her. What a nice feeling that must be to have that confidence.

Patricia broke up with Gary after a few months, but still Tom and I kept in touch with each other and every Fourth of July he invited us to that house for barbeque. That was just about the only time I saw Tom and his family, because Tom and Laura lived in a city outside Los Angeles. I loved being around Tom and his family and whenever we met, we always had a great time.

After living with Chrystal for about a year, we were getting on each other's nerves and I felt that I needed a break from her. I loved Chrystal as my friend and actually she was more like a sister to me, but we could not live together and the only way for us to remain friends, was for me to move out.

Mimi's and Patricia's friend Susanne needed another roommate, as Ellen, Susanne's previous roommate was moving in with her boyfriend Trey. Both Susanne and Ellen were also from Sweden as well. I called Susanne and told her I was interested in sharing the apartment, and just like that it was a done deal, I could move in. We took Ellen's name off the lease and replaced it with mine. I was happy to move out from Chrystal's and I think our friendship grew stronger because we made that separation. Susanne only had a one-bedroom apartment and as her boyfriend Roy was staying there most of the time, I had my bed in the living room. The arrangement was working well and Susanne even joined us when we went to the clubs. We took turns at being the designated driver.

Mimi, Patricia and I planned a trip to Las Vegas. I remembered the first and only trip to Las Vegas with Catia's people and how disappointed I was. This time would be different. Mimi, Patricia and I had the best time and that is when I understood why Antione and his friends appreciated their getaway Las Vegas trips so much. When we got back I was so exhausted and happy to be back, but it was definitely worth it.

Four months after I'd moved in with Susanne, I could not stand Roy because I thought he was 'using' Susanne, much less live in the same apartment with him. Mimi, Patricia and I decided and agreed to try to get an apartment, just the three of us. We found a two-bedroom apartment a few streets down from where I lived with Susanne and although none of us had a social security number, the management accepted our application. I had my own bedroom while Mimi and Patricia shared the other bedroom. I went into the management office at Susanne's and had them remove my name from the lease. I did not want any problems anywhere that might involve my name, plus I did not trust Roy at all. The apartment manager told me to keep them in mind if I needed another apartment in the future, because they would love to have the opportunity of renting to me again.

I was excited to have our own apartment with the three of us living together. All three of us, Mimi, Patricia and I, went off to Ikea to get things to furnish our home. We had not yet settled in when we started to plan our house-warming party. The invitation list had everybody we knew and some that we had just met. The list had a total of forty-six people and our house-warming party was a success. The three of us had started to get tired of clubbing, plus the flirting that never lead anywhere. There was a lot of talking but nothing happened, so we slowed down the partying to a few times per month.

Love found me

After working all day I needed a good workout so I headed to the gym. It was Friday night September 20, 2002. The girls had plans to go out but I wasn't up for it. So I spent some more time at the gym and while doing my cardio, I could feel the stress and tension being released; it felt so good.

It seems like it was always the same thing when we would go out and I was tired of the guys and their games. I was done playing around and I was ready to get into a committed relationship, but of course it takes two. I tend to fall too easily, was too free with my emotions and either that scared him or I got scared myself and would quickly cut him loose. Plus it seemed like I always would run into these jerks.

This time I was just sitting on the mat stretching when I saw this handsome Black personal trainer sitting by his desk doing paperwork. He looked up and when our eyes met, he smiled as always and said hello. He was so handsome, especially when he smiled and his eyes lit up. He was kind of short, had braids, a very nice body with arms the size of my thighs and he had the warmest brown eyes I had ever seen. I called him over and said,

"I really like your braids and the beads."

He looked surprised and smiled,

"Thank you. My name is Mark by the way," he said and reached out his hand.

"Hannah," I said and shook his hand, "Nice to meet you Mark."

Mark sat down by me on the mat and we talked about this and that while I did my stretches. Mark and I talked and talked just about everything until his last client arrived and it was time for me to go up to the second floor and start with the weights. He seemed to be such a nice guy and he had a warm personality. I had a really good workout and when I was done and got all my things together, Mark was back sitting at his desk and when I passed by I smiled saying,

"Bye Mark."

"Hey Hannah, are you done?"

"Yes I am."

"Can you hold on for a minute while I get my things? I'll walk you to your car."

"Sure."

The gym had a cabinet with different postcards on the wall and I read those while I was waiting. One of the postcards said **"Right when you thought you'd never find Mr. Right......",** and those words brought an even bigger smile to my face.

"Are you ready kiddo?"

I turned around and Mark was standing close by me; so close I could smell his cologne. He grabbed my workout bag from my hand and we talked as we walked out to the parking structure. I put my things in the trunk and Mark asked if I had any plans for the night.

"No nothing. I'm just going home to relax. What about you?"

"Same here. I'll probably rent a movie and just relaxing too."

"Nice."

"If you want to, you can come over to my place and watch the movie with me," Mark said.

I looked at him and felt my defenses waking up.

"Ah, let me think about it while I go home and take a shower. Give me your number and I can call you when I get home."

I would love to see him but I was so tired of all the bullshit and game playing. That was the reason I was hesitating when Mark asked me. He handed me a piece of paper with his name and number.

"Sure here is my number."

"Okay, I will call you soon and drive safely home ok?"

Mark leaned forward and gave me a soft but firm hug before he left. I had a big smile on my face when I got home. Patricia and Mimi were home too and the first thing I said as soon as I opened the door,

"Hey you know what? The cute Black trainer at the gym, the one I've been telling you about, I got his number today. His name is Mark and he wants me to come over and watch a movie with him tonight."

"And you said, what?" Patricia asked with a smirk.

"That I would call him after I took a shower."
"So are you going?"

"I want to but I don't know."

"Why not Hannah?" Patricia said.

"Girl, you know I'm just tired of guys for the moment, and to go home to his place is even worse. It is easier for things to happen if we are alone than if we are out somewhere. You know what I mean,"

I said over my shoulder as I walked into the bathroom to take a shower.

While in the shower, I deliberated with myself, should I go or not! I still hadn't made up my mind as I picked up the phone and dialed Mark's number. When I heard his soft voice I made up my mind and thought, *'what do I have to lose if I go?'*

"Have you decided if you want to come and watch a movie with me tonight?"

I heard how happy he sounded when I answered him,

"Yeah I'll stop by for a minute."

Mark gave me directions to get his house and it was only ten minutes from where I lived. I got dressed, black pants, a black long-sleeved shirt, just a little mascara and I was ready to go.

"Bye girls and have fun when you go out tonight. Be safe."

I got two big smiles back and the last thing I heard was "you have fun tonight girl!", before I closed the door.

Mark and I watched one of the movies he had at his house and we just talked. He was very sweet, not like any other of the men I had met. Mark was sincere and genuine and we had a great time. As we talked, I found out Mark was my age, he had two daughters with two different women. He had a few siblings. His mother had passed away when he was only fifteen years old. I gave him my condolences.

I told Mark I was sore from my workout, and he offered to give me a massage. I needed one so badly and accepted the offer. He massaged my neck and my back. I found it strange how comfortable and at ease I felt with him, no tension or fear at all. It was a different sensation, no one else ever made me feel like that. I turned my head towards him and looked into his eyes where I could see the same attraction that I felt for him. Mark lie down and put his arms around me still looking deep into my eyes before our lips met in a kiss. Our first kiss. I spent the night at his house and he held me tight the whole night.

After that we kept running into each other at the gym and I discovered that Mark beyond a shadow of a doubt, was a wonderful and genuine person. He and I saw each other at least three days a week and more when we had the chance. Of course with each passing day it became harder and harder for me to watch Mark at the gym while he was training female clients. I never told him that as I know it was my issue and ghosts from the past. I choose to trust him, and kept on working on my confidence and on my own trust issues. After all, it would not be fair or right to let Mark pay for how others had treated me in my past. My own insecurity and beliefs reared its ugly head with thoughts that any man I like could be able to love every other woman but me.

One day when Mark and I entered my apartment, Ellen was on the way out the door after been visiting Patricia. I introduced Mark to Ellen as we passed her on the stairs. When Mark put down the grocery bags in the kitchen he said,

"That girl is beautiful. Is she a Swedish bathing suit model or something?"

The old feeling of insecurity came over me and I turn around because I didn't want Mark to see the tears in my eyes as I started to feel weak. I walked into my room and closed the door, put both hands over my face and did my best to stop crying. *'Damn it Hannah. Stop being such a crybaby.'* I beat myself up again when I heard the door open and Mark's mellow voice,

"Hannah, what happened? Are you crying?"

"No, no I 'm not," but my wavering voice gave me away. Mark gently put his arms around me and turned me to face him.

"Why are you sad Hannah?"

I looked down on the floor,

"It's nothing. I just…it has nothing to do with you Mark."

"Talk to me Hannah. Tell me what is wrong, why are you crying?"

"All my life I've been told that no one can love me because I am too fat, too ugly, or whatever, and when you said that Ellen was beautiful, that same old feeling came over me and made me feel like the ugly duckling once again."

Mark tilted my head up with his fingertips under my chin and when our eyes met, a smile spread across his face.

"Hannah, listen to me. Yes, I said Ellen is beautiful. But because she is beautiful, doesn't mean that I want to be with her. I'm here with you."

I smiled back at him and embraced him. I can't keep on being this insecure. It will push Mark away. One day when I spoke to my mother on the phone, I asked

"Mom, what would you say if I told you that I'm dating a Black man?"

After I had been here in the USA for a year and a half and met Antione, I had been more and more attracted to Black men. I don't know if it was because of the way Antione had made me feel or if it was that I felt more accepted for who I was, by Black men. I didn't care what anyone else thought, it didn't matter to me anyway, but I wanted to hear my mother's reaction.

"My little angel," she said. "It doesn't matter if you are dating a purple alien, as long as you are happy."

I smiled to myself because it was the answer I wanted to hear. Mark used to call me leprechaun, and I asked him what that was. I had never heard that word before. Mark just smiled and told me I have to figure it out myself. I asked Mimi one day as Mark and I walked out of the apartment.

"By the way girl. Do you know what an leprechaun is?"

"You don't know what a leprechaun is Hannah? It's a mean ugly little green guy."

I looked at Mark and said,

"Oh, so you're telling me I'm an ugly green guy?"

"Well you're not a guy and I wouldn't call him ugly."

"Yeah, whatever dude," I smiled at him.

It sounded charming when Mark said it and that was all that mattered to me. It would take a few more months before one of Mark's best friends, Lisa, would explain to me what Mark really meant by calling me leprechaun and what the word leprechaun stands for.

Two months later, my sister called me and said she heard from a lawyer about our father's estate. I still think there was more of my dad's estate than my sister and I were told, but of course Liza denied it and thought that my sister and I were not entitled to anything from our father. I would rather have my father alive so he could see how happy I had made myself since I left Sweden and left everything behind. I know my father can see me from up above, but I would love to see his face and how proud he must be of me now.

Around the same time, my mom called and said she will come visit me at the end of December. My mother would be here December 22nd and stay until January 4th. That meant we would spend Christmas and New Year together. I haven't had a chance to celebrate the holidays with my family for the past four years. I had always loved Christmas and this year would be the best, so far, with both my mom, the man I love and my best friends under the same roof. What more could I wish for?

We had decided to have Christmas at our house and I was the only one who really wanted a Christmas tree. Patricia and Mimi thought it was a waste of money. So I went to get my own tree and ornaments.

Mimi helped me to put up the ornaments on the tree and when we were almost done, she said

"I got a Christmas gift to you Hannah, but you need to open it now."

"It's not Christmas yet girl," I smiled.

Mimi handled me the gift, "Just open it."

I opened the gift and it was two ornaments for my Christmas tree. Mimi had put the year on the bottom of the ornament and that would start me collecting new ornaments every year. I put them on the tree and laughed,

"See girls, we have the most beautiful Christmas tree in LA."

I was very happy as it was now more than two years since I'd seen my mother.

It was the night before she would arrive. I had butterflies in my stomach. Patricia and Mimi were excited for me and looked forward to meeting my mom. I knew I wouldn't get a lot of sleep for all my excitement. I went over to Mark's house, watched a couple of movies, talked and Mark gave me a massage to make me relax before we went to bed. The touch of his hands always makes me warm inside, and I thought about how lucky I was to have found him. I fell asleep around 4:00 a.m. and Mark woke me up with a kiss on my forehead,

"Snow white, time for you to wake up so you'll be on time to pick up your mother."

"No I don't need to leave yet," I replied and looked at the time. "The flights are never on time anyway."

I ended up staying at Mark's for another hour. I don't know why I was so nervous to meet my mother. I delayed some more by dragging out my routine but finally I put myself together after Mark almost kicked me out,

"You have to leave now Hannah and did you forget that you need to go home before you go to the airport."

"Oh yeah I had forgot everything about that, but it's all good."

I got up and got dressed, gave Mark a kiss and left. I got home the same time the flight was supposed to land and called the airline to see if the flight was on time. I found out the flight was 30 minutes early, so it had already landed. *'Damn I got to run,'* and jumped in the shower before I took off for the airport while I called Mark to see if he could calm me down. Mark started laughing when I told him my mother's flight was early,

"I told you Hannah to leave earlier from my house."

"Yeah, yeah I know but anyway do you want to have dinner with my mom and me tomorrow?"

"I'd love to, and sweetheart, you know I can't say no to your food."

I could hear Mark was smiling.

"I'll call you later and we'll see what time babe ok?"

"Sure and Hannah, just relax. It's your mother coming."

I was so lucky to have met a man like Mark. In the back of my mind, I started to believe there was a chance for a future for Mark and me. Mark had made me start believing there was actually "good" men out there in the world.

When I got close to LAX the usual anxiousness came over me. Every time, it's the same thing and I think it is a phobia. It's probably because in the back of my head I am always worried something would happen and they would deport me from the USA and send me back to the "hell hole". Back to Sweden and I would be back in Jared's grasp.

Even though the nightmares about Jared's insanity had gotten less than before, they still appeared a couple of times per month.

'Stop it Hannah because it's not going to happen and you will make sure of it.' I talked to myself all the time as I have so many hang ups from my past that play with my mind. I am doing my best to get rid of them and replace them with better thoughts instead. I just need to "catch" myself when the bad thoughts are coming before they take root and start to control my mind to believe the lies I had been told.

There has been a lifetime of negative people who just packed my mind and my life with negative things and caused me this insecurity. Mental and physical abuse! All the times I've heard how fat and ugly I was; that no one could ever love me, especially if I didn't lose weight and that I could never do anything right. No wonder my mind was all screwed up! Now that I am healing and now know nothing of that is true, I have to change my thinking to right, positive thinking, but it is not easy. I truly know in my heart those negative things are not true, that it was just that Jared brainwashed with his constant repeating it, but it seems like my mind just won't let it go. After all, I've heard all this bullshit and believed it for so many years, in fact, since I was a little girl. Now when I'm about to turn 33 years old, it's about time I figure out how to train my mind to see how it *really* is.

Like my father told me 3 years ago before he passed away, I know the difference between right and wrong, to trust myself that I'll make the decisions that are right for *me*, and I know those things Jared said and I've heard all my life, were nothing but lies.

At the airport, I waited for 20 more minutes before I saw her. Then I ran the few steps to greet mom. She let go of her luggage and embraced me firmly as she stroked my hair. Same as before, our tears fell as we stood there in the middle of everybody, just hugging each other. But we didn't care. I was so happy to have her here again. We went straight home and the apartment was empty. Patricia and Mimi weren't home yet.

"Your apartment is so nice Hannah." Mom said as soon as we entered the apartment. I was proud of everything I had achieved since I came to the US. After all, I came to this country with only $250 in my pocket after being forced to escape my home country to save my life. Three years later I have a full time job, my own car and my own apartment. Well I had two roommates but I paid half the rent so it was partly my own. I had a right to feel proud of myself!

My mother arrived December 22nd and the following day I introduced Mark to her and he came over for dinner that night. My mom and Mark got a long very well from the very beginning and my mom who doesn't think she can speak English, talked with Mark like she had known him forever.

In Sweden, we celebrate Christmas on the 24th of December and so we decided to do the same here at our house. I was very excited when I woke up the morning of Christmas Eve and I was the first one to get up. I started to gather things for our meal as I admired how good my tree looked. *'See Hannah, you've finally got that nice and quiet life you dreamed of.'*

I called the Svenssons to wish them a Merry Christmas and Pauli told me how exciting their Christmas had been as this was Wendy's, (their youngest daughter) first Christmas. I told Pauli how happy I was that my mother and I would be celebrating the holidays together. I also told her that even though I had to escape Sweden because of her brother, I was happy that we were still close like sisters.

Pauli said that Jared had been acting up with them also and that earlier in the year, he come to their home and had threatened his sister, nieces and nephews to life. Pauli said she felt very uncomfortable and decided that that was it for them, Pauli and Ron, they were done with Jared. She told him to stay away from their family, and if they heard or found out that Jared is trying to contact the children at school or elsewhere, she would not hesitate to call the police on him. This is Jared's own sister! So Pauli informed her kids' schools, the neighbors and any and everyone around them. She let them know they should call the police immediately if they saw Jared anywhere around their neighborhood.

I know many people have told me that Jared has probably forgot about me a long time ago as it's been years since I left Sweden. However, I know better, I know him well, he won't let go and won't forget, not until he gets his revenge. Jared has patience when it comes to "pay back time" and I think as he had told me many times, he would wait it out even if it took 10 or 15 years. I always got confirmation one way or another. Either through my mom who would call and say that Jared has been calling her, or that he sent a Christmas card, or in some way made mom aware that he was still around. That is Jared's way of reminding me that, I can run but I'll never be safe from him.

When people said things like that it made me frustrated! They have no clue what kind of psycho I was dealing with or talking about. Pauli is still baffled that Jared had the nerve to go to her house and threaten her family.

"Pauli, I believe anything when it comes to your brother. Remember, I lived with him for almost fifteen years."

After speaking with all of the Svenssons, we hung up. Since coming here to the US and getting the chance to start my new life, I appreciate all the little things other people might not even think about. Just waking up and having a quiet moment by myself. Having the freedom to choose what I want to do, to speak my mind. It is an extreme relief -no one who wakes me up in the middle of the night because he can't find a paper which is right in front of him; or simply just because he wants some company even though he is well aware that I need to get up early in the morning to go to work. These small things are precious to me. I get warm in my whole body at that thought and I promised myself that life can only get better because I have already seen and experienced the worse.

By now, mom joined me in the kitchen and we enjoyed each other's company as we chatted and cooked together again. Mimi had a part-time job which she wasn't too excited to go to, but it was a source of income.

About two months after I'd met Mark, Mimi was more cheery than I had seen her in a long time when she got back late from work. It didn't take long until I found out why. On her way to work, some man had literally picked her up at the bus stop while she waited for the bus. This fellow, Jeff, had stopped and offered her a ride to work. I would have expected Patricia or me to accept a ride, but never Mimi as she was the one of the three of us, that played her cards safe. But Mimi was late for work and accepted the ride. She said that Jeff asked her out to dinner and they had exchanged phone number and had set a date before he dropped her off at work. The two are inseparable since that day. I was happy for Mimi that she also had met a nice man that she really liked, and Jeff seemed to be a great man.

We all helped in getting everything ready for our dinner. Mimi was going to see Jeff but promised to return to spend some time with all of us here at the apartment. Ellen joined us later in the afternoon. We all had a wonderful time. We ate good food and had a few drinks while we chatted about sex, guys, relationships and life. I couldn't help but think that '*back in Sweden I used to watch Friends and wish that I would have that kind of friendship. Look at me now, it all became true!*' When I went to bed on Christmas Eve 2002, I was so happy and felt almost complete.

I took my mom around LA for shopping and to meet some of my friends and we were invited to Ellen and Trey for a little get together on New Year's Eve. After all the shopping we had done, mom and I both had new outfits for the party on New Year's Eve. We took a taxi to their place. The party was great and my mom was very comfortable and fitted in as if she was one of us. The only one I was missing was for Mark to be there with us. We drank champagne and Glögg, a Swedish Christmas drink, all night. At midnight after the toast, I thanked God for blessing me with everything I now had in my life; For my family and friends, who had become my family, and for Mark and as always, for my life.

The relationship between Mark and me developed to a wonderful friendship as we grew closer together. Five months into the relationship, we went grocery shopping and at the register Mark asked the cashier to wait as he took off somewhere down the aisle. When he returned, he had a big, pink stuffed frog under his arm. He paid the bill and we left the store. As soon as we walked out from the store, Mark handed me the pink frog and said,

"This is for you. His name is Pinky."

"I love him, thank you."

I held the frog in front of me so I could look at him, and in Pinky's hands he held a big, pink heart that said, "**I Love You**." The warmth I felt within my heart was indescribable. Something I had never felt before and it made me somewhat confused. Mark drove home and I had Pinky in my lap. Later that evening, after Mark left, I showed Pinky to the girls. Mimi raised her eyebrows as she said,

"It seems like things are getting serious between the two of you Hannah."

"Maybe. I mean, I like him a lot, but I don't know how Mark feels about me. He doesn't want a commitment, and he hasn't told me that he likes me. So I don't know."

"Girl," Mimi smiled now, "look what Pinky's heart is saying." She shook her head, "Hello Hannah. Wake up."

I had thought about it too, but I don't want to assume that a man like Mark, likes someone like me and then get hurt if he doesn't. I had done that before, thought someone really had feelings but didn't tell me, and then found out, it was nothing. That stuff hurts and hurts bad.

Mark had the nicest body I had ever seen. Could he like a chubby girl like me? How could I know if Mark had feelings for me if he doesn't tell me? I know Mark loved to hug me, kiss me, hold me and touch every inch of my body. Especially those places I felt the most ashamed of but when Mark touched them, somehow they didn't feel bad anymore and I started to accept my body. Still when it comes to emotions, I was definitely insecure, and couldn't or wouldn't allow myself to believe someone, a man like Mark, liked me unless they told me so.

A place to call my own

When Mimi told us, she was going back to Sweden to make arrangements to begin her studies here in the America, and that she would move in with Jeff when she came back. I decided that I wanted to stay in our apartment but Patricia couldn't afford half of the rent for a two-bedroom and I didn't need a two bedroom apartment all by myself. So, it was time for me to find another place. I went apartment hunting. I checked the LA Times every day, but when Mark and I went looking at them, none of them suited me and I was feeling rushed. I needed to find something, but it was not easy because I don't have a social security number.

I was passing by the complex where Susanne and I had lived before Mimi, Patricia and I got this apartment, and there was a vacancy sign. The manager of that complex, Julie Ann, had told me when I moved out to keep her in mind, if I ever needed another apartment because we were prompt with the rent and were good tenants, and she would love to have us as tenants anytime. I checked in at the office and there was a vacancy, a one bedroom vacancy, and in live-in condition. It was an upstairs apartment and as soon as Jolie Ann opened the door I thought, '*yes this is the one I want.*' The apartments are spacious and have plenty of closet space. I just loved it. There was another girl who had looked at it so she has first choice to get it if she wanted it.

"Please let me know, if the girl doesn't want it. I do."

The following day, Julie Ann called to say, the girl had agreed to take the apartment, that she wished me good luck to finding something soon. I was disappointed but I had to keep looking. Three days later, I still hadn't found a place when Julie Ann called me.

"Hannah it's Julie Ann. Have you had any luck finding an apartment yet?"

"No not at all."

"You see the girl who wanted the apartment didn't pass the credit check and I wonder if you're still interested?"

"Yes, I am very interested."

"Good, then I will process your application and I'll get back to you within two three days, okay?"

"Thank you Julie Ann, I really appreciate your thinking of me. I love the place."
"You are very welcome. Have a good day."

We hang up and I started to feel excitement and had to talk myself into calming down as the place wasn't mine yet. The three days that followed, I walked around tense and when my phone rang, I jumped, wishing it would be Julie Ann. When she eventually called I was so nervous when I answered the phone.

"Hey Hannah, this is Julie Ann from Casa Del Mar, how are you?"

"I'm great thanks, how are you?"

"Oh I'm fine, thanks for asking. I have some good news for you. The apartment is yours."

I couldn't help it, but I started to laugh out loud,

"Are you kidding me, are you kidding?"
"No Hannah. We are very happy to welcome you back here."

"I am happy too. Thank you so much. I'll be up tomorrow to sign the contract."

"Sounds great, I'll see you tomorrow then. Bye Hannah."

Both Mimi and Patricia were home and I turned around, jumping up and down, "I just got my first apartment!" I couldn't wait to tell Mark but I decided to wait until everything was done and I had signed the contract. I started to pack my things that same night. This was such good news for me. For the first time in my whole life, I would be getting my own place, my own apartment.

The following day after I had dropped Sarah at school, I stopped by at the management office and the contract was ready to be signed. I paid the deposit, signed all the papers and Julie Ann told me the move-in date was the 15th, but they just needed to fix one more thing in the apartment. So I could move in on the seventh of February, which was in two days. This was awesome! Just in time for my birthday. Julie Ann gave me the keys and as soon as I left the office, I stopped by at LA Fitness where Mark worked. It was around 12 noon and he was just done with one of his clients. When I saw Mark, I studied him as I walked towards him but he hadn't seen me yet. He was running his hand over his braids, as he did when he was tired. As Mark put away the weights I sneaked up behind him, and jiggled the keys in front of his eyes.
"Guess what?"

I had a big grin on my face and I couldn't stop smiling even though I tried to. Mark turned around, and he was so close. Even though he was sweaty from the workout, he smelled so good. Mark's eyes were glowing of warmth when he smiled at me,
"Did you get it?"

"Yeah I did, and I can move in the day after tomorrow."

Mark picked me up and swung me around, "Congrats Hannah. I am so happy for you."

When he held me tight like that, my heart started to beat faster. I wanted to kiss him right there, but he was still at work so I held back. I was getting serious. I tilted my head and with a sweet tone I asked,

"Can you help me move over the weekend if you have time?"

"Yes of course I'll help you. Leprechauns are too small to carry the big furniture themselves," he giggled." Will anyone else be around?"

"I'm not sure. Maybe Patricia, because we are going to move her things over to Ellen and Trey's at the same time."

"OK, I'll see if Dirk has time to help, otherwise we'll work it out ourselves."

"Yeah, I don't have too many things and nothing really heavy. Me and the girls moved it to where we live now, so you guys.., we'll be fine for sure."

The two days that followed, we packed and divided up the few pieces of furniture that we had collected. On the Saturday morning while Mark was working, Patricia and I got the truck and started to load it with everything we owned. My things went in first because my place was the last destination, so when Mark came over, we were already packed and ready to leave.

First, we dropped all Patricia's things at Ellen and Trey's place. Patricia would rent their loft and when we were done unloading the truck, Patricia asked if we needed her help with my things.

"No thanks, Patricia, we can manage it, the two of us."

The unpacking went quickly and after we dropped off the truck I asked,

"Do you have time to stay, Mark?"

"Only for a few minutes, I wish I could stay longer, but I'm going to pick up my daughter and get her some new shoes so I'll have to go soon."

During that short visit, Mark and I went around the house making suggestions of where to place the few pieces of furniture that I owed. As we stood in the living room looking at the view from there, Mark put his arms around me and gently pulled me close to him. I wrapped my arms around his waist while rubbing his back with my fingers and we meet in a kiss. That day, the very first day in my own first apartment, felt as if this was a beginning of something new. Something I never had experience, only dreamed of, before. It was a very calming feeling to know that no one would be coming in to my place without my knowledge. I was at my house, my home, unpacking boxes and moving furniture around, and just enjoying being all by myself. I had a big grin on my face, thinking of how blessed I was. I was very pleased with myself.

A few weeks later when I telephoned Mark I told him,

"Something is happening Mark. I just don't like you any more; I am falling in love with you."

There was silence from the other end of phone, and I thought I had messed it up. *'Now Mark got scared. Stupid me, why can't I just be quiet? Why do I always have to put my cards on the table? Now I scared him away.'* But then, I heard him say,

"Hannah, I want you to know something." I didn't like that statement, I felt scared but he continued, "Not everyone can talk about their emotions and how they feel as easily as you. I just want you to keep that in mind, babe. Okay?"

His voice was filled of tenderness and the attraction was obvious even on the phone. I was so relieved, "Yes I know Mark."

The next time I saw Mark, he came over and it was as if something had changed for the better between Mark and me. That night while making love, it was more intense and emotional. Our intimate touching of each other was more passionate than ever before. The following morning before Mark left, I gave him a key to my apartment. I thought it was time to trust our relationship and move forward slowly.

A few weeks after, I was having a horrible, horrible feeling in my gut. A feeling that Mark was going to be a dad again! He had two daughters already and I tried to ignore the feeling, but the thought or feeling wouldn't leave me. It was too solid, too deep. *'Is Mark seeing someone else, beside me? If he is, why did he give me Pinky?'* I just knew I had to find a way to ask him, without it sounded like I was accusing him. I just had to know. When we talked that night, as we did most evenings when we weren't together, I said,

> "Hey, I had an awful nightmare last night, and when I woke up, it felt so real so I have to ask you. Are you going to be a father again?"

> "No absolutely not Hannah. You can relax."

I smiled, "Good, it was a horrible feeling."

I shook my head when we hang up, telling myself, *'stop being so paranoid Hannah,'* but the feeling in my stomach just would not disappear. A few weeks later after a shower, I felt that my breasts were more sensitive than normal. *'Why is that? Maybe it's time for my period to come,'* I thought to myself. I never knew when I would get it, because my period has not started regular, not yet. I was also feeling kind of nauseous. I was having issues with food, every time I smelled something, fragrance or food, it made me want to puke. *'What is going on? I can't be pregnant, or can I?'*

I thought about all those times when Jared and I had tried for me to get pregnant and when we had done IVF, without success. So by now I thought that I couldn't get pregnant. When these feelings didn't leave but got worse, I bought a pregnancy test for a "just in case." After I woke up the following morning and went to the restroom, it was time to take the test. I read the instructions and followed it step by step, and then just waited. I was so nervous and those three minutes felt like three hours. My legs were shaky as I walked back in to the bathroom to get the result. I couldn't believe what the test showed, I was pregnant! We were pregnant! I started to cry with happiness and with fear. What am I going to do? I had to talk to someone, so I called Mimi.

"Are you sure the test was positive Hannah?"

"Yes I am."

"Are you going to tell Mark?"

"Yes, of course. Mark has a right to know."

"Well start with that and you'll work it out from there."

While I was getting ready for work, I thought for myself, *'I better buy another test on my way home today. Maybe this one was wrong.'* I couldn't get the thought out of my mind the whole day, the thought that I may be pregnant; *'maybe I was going to be a mother.'* The day passed by very fast and on my way home, I stopped by at the drugstore and got another test. Well actually I got a two pack. That second test showed the same result as the first; two days later, I took another two tests. I couldn't believe it was true. I was carrying a little embryo, a little baby, a mix of Mark and me. Now that I knew it was true, I made an appointment to see a doctor. I still haven't told Mark, but I would after the visit to the doctor.

The day came and as I walked through the hallway to the doctor's office, I felt excitement, but I was nervous at the same time and I felt so little, so lonely. This was supposed to be a happy moment. Don't get me wrong, it was happy, but both of us did this together, made a baby and I wished Mark was here with me. I blamed myself for not telling him yet, but I wanted to be sure before I told him. And I was worried about what he was going to respond too.

The nurse called my name and showed me into a room, where she told me the doctor would be in soon. I got undressed and sat down on the chair, and when the doctor came in and was going to shake my hand, my hands were shaking.

"I'm sorry, I am just a little nervous," I apologized with something that was supposed to be a smile, a nervous smile.

"That's okay, it's normal." Dr. Edison did an exam and said, "Congratulation Ms. Bonde, you are pregnant, but it is very early."

He measured and checked when I had my last period etc., to get the due date.

"Well it seems like you will have a Christmas baby. Your baby is due Christmas Day, December 25th."

I got dressed again and when I left the doctor's office, I was very, very happy. A baby, due on Christmas Day 2003. *This is going to be the best Christmas ever,'* I thought while I got in the car and headed towards my job. Now I just have to tell Mark, and that was something I was concerned about. What if Mark said that he doesn't want it or that I have to do an abortion? *'Come on H, Mark would never tell you to have an abortion. Mark valued all living things, and wouldn't even kill a snail.'* He could tell me that he didn't want to have anything to do with our baby, but he'd never tell me what to do. *'I can take care of the baby by myself if that would be necessary.'* But what's really worried me was that I thought I might have to go back to Sweden, which would never be safe for either me or my baby. *'I would never put my baby through that hell.'* Just thinking of that got me to really panic. *'I can't go back! But what if I don't have a choice?'* I spoke to Mimi, and she told me the same thing,

"You know how expensive everything is in this country, schools and just everything. You have a much better coverage back home."

"Mimi, I am already home," I told her.

The rest of the day I was going back and forth in my head, over what options I had. That it wouldn't be safe for neither our baby nor me, if I went back. Yes all the social benefits are better in Sweden, but I wouldn't have a life. Just thinking of moving back, gave me the same old feeling I used to have when I lived in Sweden. A feeling of emptiness, fear and that I just existed, but that I didn't really had a life. *'No, I can never move back. Jared would kill both me and my baby.'* I went home after work. *Tomorrow, Saturday, I would go the gym and I will tell Mark that I am expecting our baby.'* I called my mother,

"Hey mom, how are you?"

"I'm okay, just a little depressed. You know how it is with my money situation and my health is not that good."

I wasn't surprised. Almost every time we talked, my mother had something to complain about.

"Maybe this will cheer you up. Are you sitting down?"

"Yes I am."

"I might have to move back to Sweden, I'm pregnant. You are going to be a grandmother." My mom was quiet for a second before she said,

"What are you telling me? Where would you live? You can't live here. You know how very small our apartment is."
Just the reaction I could expect from my mother, and a lonely tear slowly started down my cheek. I wiped it away, *'now if ever, you need to stay strong Hannah,'* I told myself.

"Don't worry about that mom, I will figure something out. I got to go, but I'll talk to you later, okay?"

"You know I'm happy for you my angel, right?"

"Yeah sure,"

I nicely cut her off, as I was too sad to even talk with her anymore. I felt so lost. I called Chrystal as I needed to find some comfort. Chrystal is like a sister to me and she knows a lot about my past, including how my mother is.

"Hannah, if worst comes to worst, I know my mother and father would be happy to welcome you and the baby to their house in Stockholm."

Again my tears start, "I can't go back Chrystal. But it's nice to know that someone cares. I'll keep that in mind, if worst comes to worst."

I fell asleep on the couch which I almost do every night now, and when I woke up it was 3:00 a.m. I got up and went into the bedroom. The day after as I drove to the gym, I thought about the best way to tell Mark the news. I didn't see him downstairs, so I went upstairs and he was with a client. I walked over to him. There was a big smirk on Mark's face when he saw me,

"Hey little leprechaun, what's up?" he said and gave me a hug.

"When you are done working, I need to talk to you Mark. Can you please let me know before you leave?"

Mark looked at me as if he was trying to read my mind,

"No problem Hannah, I'll let you know."
I went downstairs again, into the room where they were holding classes. I got on a spinning bike then I saw Mark coming down the stairs. He saw me and came over.
"Hannah, you can't do things like that to me."

I got the old negative feeling in my lower stomach when someone blames me for something and I don't know what I've done. Bad anxiety!!

"What did I do?"

"Tell me we need to talk when I'm with a client. It distracts me for the rest of the session. Now what did you want to talk about?"

I looked at him,

"Can we talk after?"

"No, talk to me now Hannah."

'Ok here we go,' I thought and said,

"I might have to go back to Sweden, Mark."

Now when Mark opened his mouth and responded, he sounded frustrated,

"Why would you have to go back and risk your life? You don't want to go back, you've told me."

I looked down on the floor, almost whispering because my voice wouldn't carry, "It's not that I want to, but I might have to. I am pregnant." Now I'm looking him straight in his beautiful eyes, *"We* are pregnant."

Mark turned around and made the familiar movement of dragging his hand over his braids, he looked back at me.

"When did you find out? Are you sure?"

"Yes Mark, I am sure. I've been to the doctor and got it confirmed. Our baby is due December 25th."

"I can't think now. Let's talk about this later Hannah."

"Yeah sure, we can talk about this later."

Mark left and now I was upset and couldn't focus, so I went home. I started to feel guilty for being pregnant, even though it takes two. I did not end up in this situation by myself. For two weeks, Mark acted in a way as if he was avoiding me, but I gave him his space. I understand that Mark needed space but knew he would bring it up when he was ready to talk about it. Mark started to come around again, and things seemed to be getting back to normal between us, even though neither of us mentioned the baby. I had been thinking about the baby, about what I was going to do, and the decision I made was to stay in the US and work out whatever might come my way. I had already told the Fishers who didn't seem to have a problem with my being there with a baby. Their support was appreciated and felt great. *'How come everyone else supports me, but my own family?'* I was happy and already started to plan. Some people told me to slow down, but there was no time to waste, I thought.

Now I regret I didn't listen to them because one night a few weeks later, 3:00 a.m., I got an indescribable pain in my lower stomach. I was tossing and turning in bed, couldn't lay straight. All I could think was, *'my baby! What is happening?'* I was by myself and something was terribly wrong with my stomach. About an hour later, I felt as if my period started. I squeezed my legs together, trying to stop it from happening. It didn't work. I went to the bathroom and saw blood. As my tears fell, emptiness filled my heart. It was as if I cried out my heart. *'Hannah, sometimes things like this happen, but it doesn't mean that you are losing the baby,'* I tried pep talking myself, but deep inside I felt or knew it. I, of course, couldn't get any more sleep and as soon as the doctor's office opened, I was there. Dr. Edison examined me and said,

"There is nothing of the embryo left. I am so sorry Hannah."

I didn't care if people saw me crying as I walked to my car. I called Mark as soon as I could trust my voice would be strong enough.

"Hey can I call you back, I'm on the other line?"

"If you want to. I just want to let you know that there is no baby no more," I said with a voice so blank, I didn't even recognized myself. After a pause Mark said,

"I'll call you back."

My next call was to Sweden to tell my mother. While I was talking to her, Mark called me back and I switched over. I just told Mark what had happened, and he said he'd be over later and we would talk some more.

"Are you going to be okay Hannah?"

"I guess, but honestly, right now I don't know Mark. But do I really have a choice?"

We hung up and I called Anat to tell them what had happened and she told me to take whatever time off I needed to take care of myself. Anat knew it was traumatic to lose a baby because she had also miscarried. I drove home even though I shouldn't have. With tears falling down my cheeks, it wasn't safe and I wasn't really paying attention to what was happening around me as my vision was blurry because of my crying. Fortunately, I got home safely and as soon as I closed the door, I sank down to the floor and let go of my feelings. I had never felt so purposeless before, so empty and lonely. Never!! I stayed at home that day but I had too much time to think of what had happened and it was driving me crazy. Everyone was supportive, but I couldn't eat and I couldn't sleep, I could barely function. Chrystal gave me some pills for depression and some sleeping pills, just so I could get some rest. She knew that I don't like to take medication, and I told her that I didn't need it. But the great friend Chrystal is, she didn't listen to me.

"Take these home, just in case, okay?"

So I did. There was no way I could relax and the pain got me close to panicking, I thought this emptiness would kill me. Even when Mark came over and held me, I felt empty as if I was a lost little child who couldn't find my way home. I didn't know how to handle this situation. I had never been in a position like this before and didn't know what to do. Everyone told me I'd be okay, but I wasn't so sure about it. When it didn't get better in a week, I got worried and asked Mark

"Am I ever going to feel right again?"

"Yes, you will sweetheart, and I'll do everything to put a smile back on your face."

But not even I knew what that would be. I realized that I needed something so I could at least function, so for a few days I took some of the pills Chrystal gave me. I slowly started to put myself together and started the healing process. In a couple of days, when I felt like I could function somewhat better, I stopped taking the pills because I was scared of getting addicted to any medication.

About three weeks after the miscarriage, Mark asked if I wanted to go and see a movie with his best friend, Dirk and his female friend Lisa, and of course I said yes. I was happy that Mark wanted to introduce me to his friends. Mark and I were going to meet them at Lisa's house. As soon as we got there and Mark stepped out of the car, Lisa came to him and asked him

"What's up with you man? Why don't you return my calls?"

Mark looked at me from the corner of his eye to see if I reacted, but I was cool. I understood they were friends and had met before.

"Lisa, this is my friend Hannah. Hannah, this is Lisa."

Lisa looked at me from head to toe with a 'snobby' look on her face as if to say "and who do you think you are?" I ignored it, and thought to myself, *this woman doesn't even know me.'* We drove in separate cars to the movie theatre and Mark told me how he met Lisa. He had been passing out flyers for personal training in an outdoor mall and ran into Lisa when she was on lunch break from the bank where she worked. A few weeks later Dirk told Mark how he had met this nice girl who turned out to be Lisa.

We had a pleasant time at the movies, we actually watched three movies that day. Everything went well and when I went to bed that night, I felt happier and more comfortable for the first time since the miscarriage.

Dirk was a biker for the past ten years. Mark talked about getting his motorcycle license and then he would purchase his own bike so he could ride with them. We went to the bike shop behind the gym and there it was, a dark red and silver 1200 Hayabusa, exactly like Dirk's but different color. Mark sat on it and his eyes were shimmering as they always do when he was excited and happy. There was only one problem, money. I didn't have much money but when I got home, I gave Mark $600 to help with the down payment. Hopefully he could get the rest of the money. I wished I had all of it, but I didn't and I didn't have any credit either. Mark looked at me when I gave him the envelope and I saw the admiration I'd never seen in any eyes before. I thought it was love; now I *know* it was love. I didn't hear anything about the bike the following week, and thought maybe Mark never got the rest of the money. He called me Friday,

"Hannah, I'll meet you at your house tonight when you get home so we can have dinner together, okay?"

"Sure honey, and if I'm not home when you get there, you got the key right?"

"Yeah, I do."

I came home before Mark and he called me from downstairs and asked me to come down and open the gate. He had forgotten his key. I went down to my car, grabbed my opener and when the gate is opening, Mark come rolling down the driveway on the bike. I laughed and when Mark reached me, I put my arms around him and gave him a heartfelt hug.

"So you got your bike huh? Congratulations babe," I said with silken soft voice.

"I could never have done this without you Hannah, thank you," Mark whispered in my ear.

He parked the bike behind my car and we went up to the apartment. After dinner we both were sitting on the couch watching a movie together, Mark behind me with his legs and arms around me all snuggled up. I rested my head on his muscular chest and my emotions were overwhelming. Suddenly, despite all the happiness, I started to feel anxious. A feeling as if I was going to lose him, and I felt it was important for me to tell him. So while we watched the movie, I said,

"You know Mark, I always lose the people I love, or I have to walk away. Sometimes I turn my back at them for my own good. Something always bursts my happy bubble."

Mark held me a little harder and put his chin on my shoulder,

"Why are you telling me this Hannah?"

"I don't know, but somehow I have this feeling."

"Hannah, I am not going nowhere, okay?" Mark said and gave me kiss on my neck.

It was time for him to go home. Mark told me he wasn't allowed to drive his motorcycle after the sunset with only a permit. He just wanted to see me and share the fantastic news with me. I followed him down but the motorcycle would not start. He called Dirk to come and help him, and it only took Dirk 15 minutes to get there with his truck. Dirk got it started on the hill right outside my house. He was upset with Mark for being out riding this late. Dirk told him to take the freeway home, because between the area where I lived and Mark's house, the police were always waiting to pull someone over. A Black guy on a nice motorcycle, a perfect target and Mark would be in so much trouble. Dirk came over and was talking to me while Mark was putting on his helmet,

"Hannah, Mark is more than a friend to me. He is like my little brother. Please keep an eye on him and tell him if he is doing things he's not supposed to do. I know Mark listens to you," Dirk smiled at me.

"Sure D, of course I'll do that. I didn't know that Mark wasn't allowed to be out riding after a certain hour."

Dirk got in his truck, "Call me when you get home bro, okay?" D said and turned his head towards me, "And nice seeing you again girl."

"Same to you D, and thanks."

The following week, Mark came over on the weeknights most of the time, and on the weekend, he went out with the other bikers. Mark surprised me two weeks later, he asked if I wanted to go to the movies again with D and Lisa?

"I'd love to."

When I went to pick up Mark, he had on a burgundy cashmere sweater over black slacks. *'How can I feel so much love in my heart?'* It felt like my heart would explode. Mark and I met Dirk and Lisa by the theatre. This time Lisa looked happier to see me, and I knew that she just needed to get to know me. Then she'd see and understand I'm not like most of the other chicks. When we went into the first theatre to see a movie, we were early so Lisa and D went to get soda and popcorn. Mark and I got seated, but when Lisa and D came back, they took seats further away on a row behind us. Mark put one of his arms around me so my head leaned against his enormous biceps, and he took my hand with the other. I put both of my legs over his thigh and Mark pulled me a little closer. He looked deep into my sky-blue eyes while he gently stroked my hair, slowly put some of it behind my ear and whispered,

"Do you know how much you mean to me? I really enjoy spending time with you Hannah."

In the background the theatre played Daniel Bedingfields song, **"If you're not the one**." I sucked it in by looking down on the floor for a second, and when I met his eyes again, it was as if my feelings for him reflected in his eyes. I saw the same emotions there as I felt within myself. I leaned forward until my lips met his, and I took his hand in mine, then I pulled away a few inches,

"Same here Mark"…but I got cut off when D and Lisa passed us back there and said, "get a room ya."

When we looked back over our shoulders, the four of us were cracking up. That moment is forever stamped in my heart. We watched the movie and after, sneaked in to see *Too Fast Too Furious.* Dirk and Mark were sitting behind Lisa and me, so that allowed Lisa and me a chance to talk. I told her,

"Back in Sweden, I was about to take driver license for motorcycle but I never had the chance, maybe I'll do it now, here. It looks like so much fun."

Mark tapped me on the shoulder and both Lisa and I turned our heads, Mark said with a voice filled with worry,

"I don't want you to get a bike Hannah. If something would happen to you……I couldn't take it."

My heart was ready to burst with passion for him. I took his hand and continued to talk to Lisa. She looked at me,

"Girl let me tell you one thing. Mark doesn't want you to get a bike because he is jealous. Guy's think a woman on a bike is incredibly sexy and Mark thinks so too. If you get a bike, he knows you would have too many guys chasing you.

Mark said, "Whatever Lisa! Hannah, don't listen to her."

That was the end of that discussion at that time. We ended up watching three movies again and as we were walking out, Mark stopped and bent down, picked up something and put it on top of my hand. I looked down and it was a sticker, a heart sticker, so I put it in my wallet to not lose it. I gave both Dirk and Lisa a hug and then said goodbye. We drove home in silence and Mark spent the night at my house.

The following week was strange. I still had that uneasy feeling that I was going to lose Mark and even though I tried not to, I got jealous and it made me restless. It felt as if Mark moved further and further away from me, but I didn't understand it. If that was the case, why didn't Mark talk to me. It scared me, but I did my best to ignore it. Sometimes it worked other times, not. Wednesday of that week, Mark came over and spent the night. All night he held me close to his body. As we lay near each other like that, I became a little calmer. *'It's all in my head. Ghosts from my past. I have to let it go.'* But it seemed like it was easier said than done. Thursday night I was going out with my friends and Patricia's parents who were visiting from Sweden. We had a great time and I asked if Patricia and her parents wanted to come over for dinner on Sunday. They accepted the invitation. Mark had promised to call me but he didn't, and it annoyed me. It always does when someone promises something and don't follow through as I start questioning if the person is truthful or not. Friday came and I saw Mark at the gym. We had a chance to sit down and talk a few minutes before he had to leave. I questioned him about what was wrong. About why he had changed toward me, but Mark just looked at me, somewhat baffled,

"Hannah I am digging you. I am digging you a lot. We don't have a problem, so don't create one sweetheart, okay?"

Mark smiled and that smile always have a positive effect on me, so I put my arms around him in a warm hug.

"Okay. Be careful tonight whatever you're about to get into okay?"

"Thanks, you too."

Mark left and I finished my workout and felt great when I got home. I took a hot shower and relaxed on the couch for the rest of the night. I got up early and took off to the gym again by 11:00 a.m. I didn't see Mark anywhere downstairs, but when I went upstairs there he was. Mark was his usually self, laughing about everything and at his own jokes. I did the same. Mark was amazing and was always able to make me smile at one thing or another. It was time for him to leave, but before he left, he came back up to talk to me.

"It's D's 40th birthday today so we are rolling out with the bikes."

I could see how excited Mark was and even if I was sad that I wouldn't have a chance to see him, I was happy for him. When he was happy, I was happy.

"Okay babe. Tell Dirk happy birthday from me okay and please be safe."
"I will," he said over his shoulder as he rushed down the stairs.

On my way home, I picked up groceries that I need for dinner the following day and decided to stay home the rest of the evening.

It was Sunday June 15th, Father's Day. Patricia called to see if I wanted to join them to the beach so I met them there. We stayed for a few hours, long enough for me to get sunburned. It seemed like I never learned that I have very sensitive skin. Patricia and her mother came to dinner, but Patricia's dad stayed home. It was just us girls. Everything was ready and we sat down to eat. I had made spaghetti and meat sauce, garlic bread and for dessert, we had chips and salsa. I hadn't heard from Mark since he left the gym the day before. Anyhow he called while we were eating, somewhere about 7:33 p.m. When I answered, Mark said,

"Hey baby what are you up to?"

It was so nice and hearing his voice calmed me down.

"Patricia and her mom are here for dinner and we are just sitting here talking. What have you been up to? And happy Father's Day by the way."

"Thanks. Me and Dirk went down to Long Beach yesterday and got back by noon today. We are just about to leave Friday's in Inglewood."

I knew his ex, the girl who broke his heart, lived in Long Beach and I felt a sting in my heart, but only for a second.

"Great. Did you guys have fun?"
"Yeah we did, but I miss you."

I almost fell of the chair. Mark had never said anything like that straight forward regarding emotions before.

"I miss you too," I respond with a smile.

Now I thought Patricia was going to choke on the chips and the look she gave me. A look saying, *"Did Mark really say he missed you?"* Mark woke me up again by saying,

"Hannah, I'm just going home to drop the bike at home and switch to my car. After that, I'll come over to your place."

"Sure. I can't wait to see you."

"Likewise little leprechaun."

I heard the smile in this voice and we hung up. I wanted Patricia and her mom to meet Mark just to say hello but it was now 8:30 p.m. and Mark still hadn't showed up or called. He didn't answer his phone either and although I left a message, Mark hadn't returned my call. Patricia and her mom had to leave. I called Mark again but this time I didn't leave a message. *'Why is he doing things like this?'* I felt my old insecurities creeping up on me. *'Mark is so sweet, not like any of the other men I had met, so why is he starting acting like this?'* I was really scared especially since I'd been having those bad feelings and thoughts for these past weeks. *'Is Mark with someone else? Maybe I'm just not that important in his life? Well Mark can have whatever girl he wants, so why would I be number one? No one could love me in the long run.'*

These were the thoughts running through my head. My mind was going round and round, reminding me of all the things my father and Jared had told me when I was younger that no one could love me because I was too fat and too stupid. *'What made me believe Mark could love me?'* I didn't know because he never told me. So it was likely I just wished it so. By 11:00 p.m. Mark still hadn't answered his phone so I got ready for bed, and hoped that I would calm down. I was tossing and turning. I called his number on and off, but still no answer, and then later the phone was turned off.

June 16, 2003, The reason for Marks silence

When I woke up at 6:00 a.m., I was incredibly tired as I hadn't slept well the night before. I was too concerned and upset about all this stuff with Mark. I was confused and felt everything from disappointment, sadness, anger to worry. *'Why did Mark say he was on his way over and then just not show up or answer his cell phone? I just don't get it! Mark surprised me by saying he missed me, and then just didn't care to show up. Why do I let someone play with my mind like that? Hannah, you should know by now if a man doesn't actually tell you that he has romantic feelings for you, don't assume that he has. Why can't you understand Hannah? You're still living in your dream world. Sooner or later, they all leave you. Not because you like him and he is acting as if he cares ….., maybe it's all in your head Hannah because you want him to like you … doesn't mean that he does have that kind of feelings for you.'* I close to drove myself crazy with my thoughts. *'Why am I doing this? What is wrong with me?'*

I called his cell again and it went straight to voicemail again. I didn't leave a message. *'I hope she's worth it Mark.'* What else could keep him away from me if not another woman? *'But why did Mark tell me he missed me and that he was coming over, if he knew he was going to see another woman?'* I was confused and had to focus on what I had to do for the day, before the chatterbox in my head started up again with these questions and speculations and no answers. *'Shower, get dressed and go to work. Oh yeah, I'll write Mark a note and put on his trainer shirt that I had washed for him.'*

I knew that Mark had scheduled his first client at 10:00 a.m., and he had to stop by here before that to pick up his shirt. The first note I wrote in anger. When I got to work and I was more calm, I felt badly about it, and went home hoping that Mark hadn't been there yet so I could rewrite it. The note and the shirt were still there, proving that Mark had not been here. I threw the first note away and wrote a new one that said, **'I missed you last night, what happened? There is lunch you can take to work and hopefully I'll see you later. Have a wonderful day.'** I put that message on top of his shirt and smiled just thinking of Mark. *'Yeah I do miss you so much.'* I felt so calm when I went back to work. I was happy that I had the chance to write another note. After all, Mark didn't need any stress from me and deep down inside me, I knew there must have been a good reason why he didn't come to see me.

The look in his eyes when I was around and the way he touches me, I am sure he couldn't lie to me. He had strong feelings for me.

Mark's phone was still off and I kept calling once every half hour. At 1:00 p.m. the phone was back on and I left a message when he didn't pick up. At 2:00 p.m., Mark still hadn't returned my call and I called again. A woman answer and I was surprised but asked,

"Hey is Mark there?"

"Who are you?"

"Excuse me, but who are you?"

"I'm his baby's mama. Who are you?"

I know it was his youngest daughter's mom, her name was Lashana. Mark had been telling me about her and she was staying with him for the time being, she and her seven kids, so I just responded,

"I'm a friend to his so can I just talk to Mark?"

"What nationality are you? Are you Asian? Have you been to Disneyland together?"

I started to be irritated with all these questions,

"It doesn't matter where I'm from. Is Mark there or not?"

"No he's not. Mark died last night."

My heart stopped and I struggled to get some air, and whispered,

"Can you say that again?"

"Mark died in a motorcycle accident last night." Lashana repeated.

My tears started to fall and I tried to remain calm. It must be a mistake.

"Are you kidding me?" I couldn't think of anything else to say.

"No I am not, and now I want to know what kind of relationship you had with him?"

What Lashana told me was ridiculous. I talked to Mark last night and he was going to come over, but he never came …. but dead!? No, not Mark. It must be a horrible mistake. I did my best to think straight. Maybe Lashana just said this because she was jealous and wanted me to back off. But would she say something that dreadful? Mark had told me about Lashana. It was just a one-night stand and she got pregnant, but he never had any feelings for her. The nice man Mark was, he took responsible for his actions, took care of his daughter even though he didn't wanted to commit to her mother. Lashana already had six other children, and all from different men. So when Lashana and her seven kids got kicked out from her mother's house, Mark let them all stay with him. They had now been there for about two weeks. While they were staying in Marks house, she must have realized Mark had met someone that he really cared for, but she didn't know who so now she was trying to figure it out.

"How did it happen?"

"Mark got hit by a car. But now you've got to answer my questions."

That's all I heard before I hung up the phone. I could feel the panic coming over me, but I tried to calm myself so I could think. *'Hannah, you know Lashana doesn't like you, maybe it's not true. She just wants to get you out of the picture, out of Marks life. You know Mark said she's capable to a lot of tricky things so you can't trust her. Think Hannah, try to figure out how you can find out if it's true or not.'* My mind was chaos and I couldn't see anything because my tears were falling like a waterfall. I called Chrystal to tell her what I had heard, but I didn't make any sense, I was not clear and said I'd call her back. I know Patricia was on her way to Las Vegas with her parents but I called her anyway and told her.

"Hannah I have to call you back, I'm driving okay?"

"Okay."

My mind was working full speed, trying to figure out how I could find out what was going on. I remembered his client at 10:00 a.m. I called the Fitness Club and asked for Craig, a young man who also was a trainer. We used to talk as his father was from Sweden also. Craig knew about Mark and me but as he was busy, I left a message with the front desk asking him to call me back. I asked

"Mark, the trainer, had a client today at 10:00 a.m., did he ever show up to that session?"

"I am sorry but I can't leave out information regarding our staff."

Craig called me back a few minutes later and I asked him the same question. Craig started to say he didn't know, but close to panicking I cut him short and said,

"Listen Craig. Someone told me Mark died last night and I don't know how to find out if it is true or not. Please help me."

"Hold on a second while I ask...." I heard him put the phone down and when he picked it up again, his voice sounded strained. "He never showed up to his appointment, and we haven't heard anything from him. I am truly sorry Hannah. If you hear anything, can you please let me know?"

"Of course I will Craig, and you do the same, ok?"

I called Anat on her cell phone and did my best to explain, but I was close to hysterics by this point and could not find the right words. Anat got worried but with a calm voice, she told me

"Are you sure that what the girl is telling you is true?
"I don't….How can I? I just know I can't reach Mark."

"Hannah, you need to try to figure out a way to find out if it is true or not, before you get too upset. Maybe she is just lying to you because she knows Mark's heart belongs to you."

We hung up. I had thought the same thing as Anat told me. The only way to really find out is to call the Inglewood Police Department, as TGI Fridays was the last place I knew for sure Mark had been. I got the Inglewood number from information. The whole time I was shaking and my mouth was dry when I dialed the number, a man answered,

"Inglewood Police Department, how can I help you?"

"I want to know if there was a motorcycle accident in Inglewood last night where a person was killed?" I said with a shaky, weak voice and my accent came out even more.

"Hold on for a minute and I'll connect you to someone else."

"Thank you."

Another man picked up the phone and I asked him the same question.

"Do you know where it would have been?"

"I have no clue, but somewhere around TGIF Fridays and Rodeo Boulevard in Inglewood sometime after 7:30 p.m."

I told him exactly how it was and that I didn't know who to call.

"I can't give you any information and the officer who worked last night, he'll be in here later so can you call back?"

"Sure I can, but can you at least tell me if there had been any motorcycle accident there last night?"

The man on the other side of the phone line took a deep breath and said,

"Yes, we had an accident there last night, but like I said I don't have any information about it, you have to call back."

Suddenly my whole body got ice cold and I sank to the floor, still with the phone in my hand. I closed my eyes and thought my heartbeat stopped. I couldn't feel anything. *'It's true. I just know it is.'* In a period of six weeks, I had lost the best part I ever had in my life; my baby to a miscarriage and my boyfriend in a motorcycle accident. It was as if all my emotions suddenly left me and all I felt once again, was blank, an indescribable emptiness. I had lost my whole future. I don't know how long I sat there before Anat came home, pulled me up on my feet and hung up the phone.

"Hannah is it true? Did you find out anything?"

I just looked at her with vacuous eyes and said,

"Yes it's true."

"Hannah whatever you need to do, do it. You are more than welcome to stay here if you don't want to be alone now. Take time off but if you leave, please don't drive. You are too upset now."

Anat had to go to Limores school for something and I started to call the hospitals around that area. I called Mark's cell phone again and when Lashana answered, I just asked if I could get Dirks phone number.

"Hell no you ain't getting anything before you answer my questions."

I was not going to argue with Lashana when I knew she wouldn't give it to me, so I kept on calling the hospitals. The third hospital I called was Martin Luther King and while the two others said '*No we don't have anyone with that name here,*' The nurse started to ask me questions about who I was and what relationship I had to this Mark?
I told the nurse how it was and she said,

"We can just talk to his family so you have to call them."

"Look," I said. "I don't have any contact with his family and someone just told me my boyfriend Mark is dead. I don't know who I can ask and I'm about to go crazy if I don't find out what is going on, if it's true or not. Can you please help me?"

My voice shattered and she heard how desperate I was. For the longest time, it was probably just a minute but felt like forever, the nurse was quiet and then said,

"Have someone drive you down here and I will see what I can do but you have to be here before 5:00 p.m. because I'm getting off then."

"Thank you so much, I'll be there."

It was already 3:00 p.m. and I called Ellen to see if she could drive me. I was thinking about Lisa, the girl who came with us to the movies with Dirk. I didn't know Lisa's last name but recalled Mark said she was working at a bank down in Marina Del Ray so maybe I can find her there. After debating with myself what to do and where to go, I figured I will have a better chance to find Lisa then to get down to Martin Luther King on time, so when Ellen came we headed for Marina del Rey. I was talking and talking but I don't think I made any sense to anyone at that point. My mind was going like a hundred miles per hour and my eyes were red from all crying when I walked into the first bank when we got there. Everyone was looking at me when I stepped in there and I asked a man,

"Excuse me, do you have a Black girl with braids named Lisa who works here?"

"No we don't. I'm sorry."

"Are there any more banks around here?"

"Yes, there is another around the corner here and then there is a another one on the other side of the street."

I turned around and walked out to go to the next bank when a man stopped me and asked if I was okay?

"No I'm not."

Same thing at the other bank, but no, the second bank didn't have any Lisa either. It took all my strength to not break down and let the panic get to me while Ellen drove me to the last bank. I walked in and when it was my turn, a cute girl with red hair asked how she could help me.

"Do you have a black girl with braids who works here? Her name is Lisa."

"No we don't but we have a Lisandra here. But she's not in today."

Once again, I closed my eyes and I could feel this was the right bank. Of course Lisa's not working today when her best friend just died last night.

"Can you do me a favor please?" I asked the girl.

"Sure what do you want me to do?"

"If I leave my name and number, can you give it to Lisandra and tell her to call me?"

"You can write it down here," she said and gave me a business card.

I put down my information and gave it back to her.

"Thank you so much for your help."

I turned around and went out to Ellen who was waiting in her car.

"Yeah this was it I think, but Lisa is not here today."

June 17, 2003, The wake-up call

I had slept for a few hours when the phone woke me up.

"Hello."

"Hi, may I speak to Hannah?" A woman asks with low voice.

"Speaking."

"This is Lisa, Mark's friend. You left a note at my job yesterday to call you."

Now I was wide-awake. As soon as I heard who it was, I felt the first tear roll down my cheek.

"Hey thank you for calling me. Is it true Lisa?"

"Yes it is. Dirk had called me sixteen times last night but my phone had run out of battery. I got his message yesterday morning on my way to work."

"But what happened? Was Dirk there too?"

"No Dirk and Mark had said bye at Fridays. D went towards his house and two other bikers were in company with Mark, on their way home from Friday's. A truck switched lane, Mark was about to get hit so he swirled and came over on the wrong side of the divider, towards oncoming traffic and was hit by a car on that side."

Even if I was prepared to get it confirmed, it was as someone ripped my heart from my chest. I had never felt such pain and helplessness like that before.

"Do you know if Mark was suffering Lisa?"
"He died immediately and there is nothing left of the bike. It was bad Hannah but no, he did not suffer. I told Dirk if he had your number or address, but he couldn't remember exactly where you lived. You were the only woman I had a great feeling about with Mark. The only one who was genuine enough for him, and not one of these ghetto girls. He had stopped bringing girls around me, until he met you." I was just listening to Lisa as she continued,

"We are going over to his dad's house tonight to plan what is going to happen now and I want you to be there as well. If you want, I can come and pick you up after work and we can go together?"

When Lisa stopped talking, my tears were streaming down my cheeks. '*Oh my little sweetheart. Mark must have been so scared when he realized what was about to happen, and I wasn't there. I was home, mad at him for him not showing up. The reason was that he was dead. Mark died on his way to come and see me.*'

"Yes Lisa, I would really appreciate if you can come and pick me up."

After been giving Lisa my address and decided she would call when she was on her way, we hung up. I walked around in a trance the rest of the day. In one way, I was relieved now when I got confirmation and I didn't have to question if it was true or not. The other part of me was panicking and didn't want to believe it was true. *'I am never going to see Mark again?'* I could not accept that.

When Lisa picked me up and we arrived to Mark's father's house, everybody looked towards us. Lisa introduced me to some of the people, and when Dirk saw me, he came over to hug me. Everyone was giving their opinion of what to do and where to go. I was just observing everything that was going on. We all came to an agreement that, no matter what or how we were going to work this arrangement out, Mark was not going to be cremated.

Lashana was there as well, and when she saw Dirk embrace me, I believe she put one and one together and figured out that I was the one who had called Mark's cell phone two days before. As the evening progressed she understood how much I meant to Mark. Oh, I could see that woman hated me for that.

At one point during the evening, Lashana sat down next to me while two of her teenage daughters sat down on my other side and she said to me,

"Why don't you just take off and disappear from here? It'll be a smart move."

I just looked at her but didn't say anything. Nothing could scare me anymore, and definitely not a woman. I told Lisa about it when she took me home and she got extremely upset and told me not to worry because Dirk would make sure Lashana won't come near to me anymore. That evening was the beginning of a great new friendship between Lisa and me. Lisa and Dirk took me under their wing and kept me updated with what was happening and made sure I was a part of it.

The following evening when we got together for the candlelit along with praying for Mark, the bikers make sure Lashana didn't have a chance to get close to me.

My heart was broken into pieces

Mark didn't have life insurance, and to get money for his funeral, we started a collection at the gym. Dirk and Lisa contributed what they could and collected from the other bikers. I added all the money I had saved up, which was $1200 and with what we had collected otherwise should have been enough to give Mark a decent funeral. Mark's father Ernie and older brother Ernie Jr, had other plans of how to handle the situation. Mark's aunt didn't agree and there was this disagreement, if the funeral didn't go how they wanted it to, then they would not put in any money to help with the funeral arrangements.

Mark didn't deserve all that drama his family created around him when he was alive, and definitely not now that he was dead. It took nine days before the viewing and Lisa said she would not go. I had never been to a viewing before, but I had to attend because, after all this was Mark. I had to see with my own eyes that it was true, that Mark had passed and that I'd never see him again.

Lisa called me and said she had changed her mind and would be there to support me. I was nervous, my body quivered when Lisa and I walked into the mortuary. I walked by Ernie Jr and was just about to enter the room where the casket with Mark's body was, when I turn my head and in the space between the door and the wall, I saw a glimpse of Mark lying in the casket and I fainted. If it wasn't for Eric, Mark's cousin, I would have hit the floor as my legs refused to carry me. Eric held me against him and gentle escorted me into the room and sat me down on the couch.

From the couch, I could see the whole casket and I pushed Eric's hand off me and slowly walked towards the casket. I stared at Mark's lifeless body and at that very moment, all my faith and hope for a happy future left me. I guess it was now for the first time that I truly understood that Mark was dead and gone forever. I looked at Lisa and she snapped a photo of me by Mark's casket. In that photo, my eyes were just as lifeless as Mark's.

Marks family had arranged a service at the church but could not agree about how or where to bury him. It was frustrating for me and his friends as we just want him to rest in peace. The following afternoon Lisa called me to tell me that Mark's family had cremated his body and that there'll be no funeral. I just couldn't make any sense of how anyone, especially his father and brother, could be so cold hearted. They took all the money we collected and instead of giving Mark the funeral he deserved, his father took the money for himself, I guess, and cremated Marks body instead. It was the cheapest way to get this done and over with.

The family had promised us, his friends that they would not cremate Mark as we wanted his spirit to have a chance to grow as something else. For example, be a beautiful tree, as Mark had once told Dirk. When we found out Mark's body was cremated, Dirk told Lisa that he was done, that he would have nothing more to do with it. That he would always remember Mark the way he was when he left Friday's that night and then let it go.

Dirk was devastated, just like all of us, because Dirk had lost more than a friend; he had lost someone he thought of as a younger brother. Lisa, who I had become very close to, told me to let it go as well but I just couldn't. I called Mark's father Ernie and asked what the family was planning on doing with Mark's ashes. Ernie said they didn't know yet.

"So you are telling me that I won't even have a place to go visit him and talk to him?" I asked. "How do you think I can I ever go on with my life, knowing Mark don't even have a place to rest?"

When we hang up, I was upset and bothered, just thinking of them not even giving Mark peace. Yes, his family did stress him out and did not respect Mark when he was alive, but to continue the disrespect when he was dead was too much. How compassionless can people be? I telephone them again and talked to Mark's brother, and negotiated with Ernie Jr,

"If you allow me to pick up Mark's ashes at the mortuary without you or your father touching it, I will buy a grave, give him a headstone and bury your brother Mark myself."

After Ernie Jr had talked to his father, he called me back and said they would agree for me to pick up the ashes. I then called Lisa and asked her to help me find a cemetery where we can bury Mark. I had never before had to do anything like that, arrange to bury someone and Lisa was from here and more familiar with where and how to make it happen. I picked up the urn with Mark's ashes and since that day, I never spoke to Mark's family again. It was in my hands now, I would make sure Mark got the peace that he needed and deserved.

It was more difficult than I thought to find a cemetery. I didn't even have the money yet, but I never gave up. Meanwhile I made a little "memorial table" in my apartment where I put the urn, a picture of Mark, a candle, flowers and a teddy bear I'd bought him. When I found a beautiful cemetery that had an open space, Chrystal loaned me the money to bury Mark. It was only Lisa, Chrystal and me there that day. I asked a priest from The Norweigan Seamanns Church if he could come and give Mark his last blessing and the priest was happy to do so. That same day I changed my cell phone number as I never wanted to hear from Marks family again.

The pain I feel was indescribable. How can life be so unfair and take away the most wonderful man I ever met, the man who was my future. When I finally met someone I actually could see a future with, God had other plans so he came and took him away from me. The last two weeks we had together, I felt like I was going to lose Mark, but at that time I thought it was to another woman. Not that Mark was going to die. I lost him, but I never lost his heart. It wasn't his choice to leave me and now I had lost all faith for my future as well. Two weeks after Mark past away, the pain in my heart was so strong and I took a piece of paper to write down my emotions.

"To my love Marquise 7-1-03

16 days without you
And I don't know what to do
Everybody telling me to stay strong
How can I when everything been so wrong
Can't believe it was your time to leave
While I'm drying another tear with my sleeve
Why did we get so little time
Our love was everything but not a crime
June 15th at 8:00 p.m. it was a Sunday
God send his angels to take you away
You called me 30 minutes before
To say "I miss you more"
"I miss you too and been doing so all day long"
You answer "You don't have to wait for
long, 'cause I'll be over later on"
You never came even if everything you said you meant
Right then you got killed in a motorcycle accident
Now I'm standing here lost and all alone
Can't accept, can't believe I'm like in a denying zone
I want to let you go and set you free
But it's just killing me
I can't, not now
I don't even know how
You're the one my lifetime soul mate
Wait for me I won't be late
I'm praying every night on my knees
And no one else can ever take your keys
It feels like someone stabbing me with a knife
'Cause MARK you're the best thing that
happen to me in my whole life.
Always in my mind & forever in my heart! With all my love, Hannah"

Now when I'm sitting here by his grave at the cemetery I
get all these flashbacks from everything we went through during our
time together. All the experiences we shared. I found out I can get
pregnant and Mark showed me that I don't need to be too scared to

trust someone and that it was safe for me to love. The most important, Mark showed me that someone could love me and love me for whom I am. Love everything about me -- my body, my soul and my heart. Mark taught me how to love myself just the way I am.

I am remembering when we went to the movies with D and Lisa for the first time and just when Mark got the bike, I told him that I was thinking getting a motorcycle license as well, and I'll never forgot what he told me. "I don't want you too. If something happens to you…..I could never take that Hannah", and now I'm standing here all by myself after losing him in a motorcycle accident. *What made you think I can take this better then you could have Mark?'* I whispered. *Why did you leave me?'* I felt lost. More lost than I have ever felt before and I have an unanswered question.

That was a question I will never get answered, but I will always wonder. I don't know where to go from here and what I need to do to keep my spirit up. I really don't know if I can go on. It seems like some people go through life without any drama at all, while others get it all. I mean, I've been through so much in my life, both as a child and an adult, so when I finally get the strength to break out from my past and start to build my own life in peace and harmony together with a wonderful man, the angels come and take him away. We had nine months together and partly because of Mark, my life took a new direction.

I closed my eyes when the first tear rolled down my cheek, and it hurt so much I can't find words to express just how much. I feel so helpless because I know that it doesn't matter what I do, Mark is not coming back. I will never look into his warm eyes again and now there is no one to help guide me, to encourage me, like he always did when I was going through tough times or when I was sad. He would always do something to make me smile. Of course, there were times when I thought our relationship wouldn't last, but we always worked through the little glitches and we knew we could make it work. Mark did for me what no one else has ever done.

He was there for me when I really needed someone. I am independent and can handle my own affairs. I take care of things by myself, but throughout my life I've been searching for someone who would catch me when I fall, who would be there when I needed a shoulder to cry on. Just someone to tell me that everything was going to be ok. Through it all Mark always found a way to put a smile on my face.

As I'm hugging the little teddy bear I'd bought to put his grave, I am thinking *'who's going to put a smile on my face now?'* I don't really know how to handle all these emotions that I am feeling. I'm so angry because this wasn't supposed to happen, and I miss him so much already. I don't know what to do or where to go from here. I was angry at God for being so unfair, for interrupting our love when we had just found each other, and for taking both our baby and Mark away from me. Had I really been so bad in this life or another to deserve this, to be lonely and have this incredible pain in my heart? Now that I have laid Mark to rest, I needed to figure out how to deal with my own heart break and move on with my life. I just don't know how. I was a jumble of thoughts and concerns. I have to pay Chrystal the money that she loaned me so I could give Mark a funeral and a nice headstone.

Friends and acquaintances were already telling me that it will be ok, that things would get better with time, and that there is a reason for everything. But no! There is no reason in the world for God to interrupt our love like this, as I asked myself over and over again, *'have I really been so unkind in my life so I deserve this?'* I know I have not. Why then, when I for the first time in my life was truly happy, why did this have to happen?

It was an unbearable time for me after this horrible trauma. I managed to work and take care of my responsibilities, paying my bills and getting through from day to day, just the everyday things. No one was going to take care of those things for me, so I had to buck up and plough through as I couldn't afford to have a breakdown in any part of my affairs. No, nothing else could go wrong. Some days I walked around feeling numb all day. Other days, I thought I was going to die. I couldn't imagine that I would get through this to be strong again. I was impatient and snapped at the smallest of things, things I had never given much attention before. I just wasn't feeling like myself anymore. I believed I was going to have a nervous breakdown, but again I knew that wasn't an option for me.

In mid-2003, Tony and Laura moved back to Los Angeles and we were in communication more than we had been for several months. After Mark passed, Lisa and I found comfort in each other's company and we became good friends. Lisa explained to me what Mark meant by giving me the nickname, Leprechaun.

Leprechaun stands for "Lucky charm", and that was how Mark had felt when he met me. I was his lucky charm. Lisa's family treated me as if I belonged in their family. If Lisa was invited somewhere, I was too. I spent Thanksgiving, Christmas and New Year's Eve with Lisa, her family and friends. They used to call me, "the white chocolate chip in the chocolate chip cookie," as I was the only white person around them. Lisa's nephew jokingly asked me, "Hannah, are you sure you're not Black? Maybe God just forgot to give you the color." Another comment I heard, "She is just very light skin." It was all said with warmth and our visible differences (skin or eye color) never made a difference among us.

A year and a half later, Lisa stopped talking to me. She changed her phone numbers, and I couldn't reach her at work or on her cell, she just stopped calling me.

I went over and over in my mind if there was anything I'd said or done, but I couldn't find any reason for her to make that decision and discontinue communication. Lisa's silence and all my questions were causing me much confusion. This was another loss for me, and it took a lot of strength and struggle to let it go. If only Lisa would have given me an explanation, but she never did. And up to today I still do not know the reason.

One who was a true support at this time were Tony, and he did everything to help me move on with my life and let it go. I know he was right but one thing I did not understand was how could Lisa just erase me from her life? Like I too was dead?

At the end of 2003, I felt that I needed a change in my life and I decided to change jobs. I felt that my depression after Mark's death and my lack of patience was having a negative impact on the kids. Sarah was only six years old at the time and she knew how sad I was because she saw me crying many, many times. I just couldn't keep my sorrows hidden. It was tearing me apart. One day when Sarah and I were out driving, she said,

"Hannah, you are so sad because your boyfriend died, right?"

"Yes Sarah that is why I am sad." With a child's innocence she asked

"So why don't you just get another boyfriend?"

I couldn't help but smile,

"I wish it was that easy Sarah."

I stopped working for the Fishers in August of 2003. The family understood, even though they were not happy with my decision to leave. While working for them, we had gone through a lot together, and maybe that's why I needed to leave. I was leaving to get a new start in every area of my life. I found another nanny position advertised in the LA Times that seemed interesting and I called.

Then I met with the mother, Judy, at her job and the interview went well. That weekend, I went up to their house in Pacific Palisades, where I met two of her sons. Sam was fourteen, and Dave was ten. I was also introduced to the two dogs, the most handsome golden retriever, I've ever seen. He reminded me of a little lion. His name was Denver. The other dog was a cute little black coca-poo named Susie. Upon my arrival at the home, Sam opened the door with Susie in his arms. He said that Susie did not like anyone outside the family.

They told me that Susie was a rescue dog and I understood that this was maybe a trust issue, even with a dog. We went on a house tour, discussed what the job was all about and I left my references with Judy. The following day Judy called me back.

"Hannah, it was very nice meeting you the other day. You have a very big fan club and my family and I would be honored to join it too. The position is yours if you want it."

"I'd love to."

When I started my new job three weeks later, in January 2004, I met Judy's husband Martin, and their middle son Mitch who was thirteen. One of the first things I noticed was that Denver, the dog, was being favored and that Susie was being less favored or ignored. I decided that I would be more even handed and share the time more evenly with the dogs. No different than I had done with Shelly and Rob, the kids, when I worked for Sue. Shelly was always the one stealing the attention from Rob with her witty personality. Then I would pay more attention to Rob and we became close.

By me loving, trusting and paying attention to Susie, she is now a friendlier little dog. She can still withdraw from some people, but she can now trust and be around people as Denver can. Susie trusts me more than she trusts anyone. If she's hurt or sad, it is me she turns to for comfort. We have become the best of friends, good buddies. Everything worked out very well. The Ashers gave me plenty of responsibility and with time, my job title changed from nanny to house manager/personal assistant.

A few months later, Tony called me and was heartbroken. Laura had broken up with him after five years; she wanted her "freedom" as she put it. Their breakup affected me because I knew both of them. At first, I didn't know what to say to either of them or what to do. But it didn't take long for me to realize which one was the true friend to me. It was Tony. I did everything that I could think of to help and to be there for Tony. We became best friends, Tony and I knew we would always be there for each other. And I made a promise to myself that I would never jeopardize our friendship. After he healed from the heartbreak, Tony finally moved on. They say there is a meaning in everything, and even though we can't understand and see it at that time, I believe there always is. After Tony got back on the dating scene, he met Linda in 2007 and he fell in love again. They are now married and I couldn't be happier for them. My "boy", my best friend, has found his soul-mate and I wish them all the luck and love in the world.

Trying to move on

It was a Friday, August 22, 2003, when Patricia, Ellen, Trey, Susanne and one of her friends who was visiting from Sweden were planning to go clubbing. They invited me along. I hadn't been out since Mark's passing. I accepted the invitation to go with them. Maybe my mind would get a break and think on something fun. I got ready but didn't really feel any excitement or drive to go out. I put on a jeans dress, high heels and a little make-up --mascara, eyeliner and lip-gloss. I had never been to that club before but the music was good and the vibe was great. After we had been there for a while, the girls and I went up on the dance floor. I noticed a tall, Black guy watching me and after a while he came over and asked to dance with me. He was about 6 foot 4. The girls were watching to see if I was okay, and I was! We sat and talked. He introduced himself as Derrick and he was 29. He seemed nice and before it was time to leave for the night, Derrick gave me his phone number and I promised to call him.

The following Monday I called and we talked for a while before we decided that I would go over to his house to watch a movie. I was emotionally drained and hadn't felt any affections since Mark passed. So for me to be there with his arms around me and fall asleep, and I slept better than I had done in months, was something. We started to see each other even though Derrick didn't want to commit to me. Two months later, Derrick told me he had something to tell me, and I got an unpleasant feeling, but said, "I'm all ears."

Derrick told me he wasn't 29 years old; that he was 33 and that he had three kids, but they were living with their mothers. Because he had lied to me about something as insignificant as his age, it should have raised a red flag. That should have clued me in that he wasn't for me, but I closed my eyes and ignored it. Derrick's then said,
"Oh that is only club talk. I didn't really expect us to become friends, but now that we are, I thought I should tell you."

'*Okay, well at least he was being honest now,*' I accepted his excuse. I also suspected that I wasn't the only girl Derrick was seeing, but here in the US people date more than one person at the time. I hoped that with time, when Derrick got to know me and understood the kind of woman I am, that he would chose to be with me. On the other hand, Derrick got jealous if I didn't answer his calls or text, or if I couldn't see him when he wanted to see me. I wasn't dating anyone else the first eight months, but then it was clear to me that Derrick wasn't going to make a decision but told me. "You are someone I want to hide from others."

What Derrick meant was easy to understand. He didn't want to commit to me, but he didn't want anyone else to have me either, to have the cake and eat it too in a matter of speaking. One day when we were just sitting and chatting about this and that, we were discussing my past and I told him I was going to write a book about my past. I had told him before about my psycho abusive ex fiancée in Sweden, and I had started to translate only a little part of my journal at that time. I showed it for him. After a few minutes, Derrick looked at me and said,

"You can't write this about him."

"Why not?"

"You make him look so bad."

I jumped to my feet, I just couldn't believe what I had heard. I looked at him sternly,

"Screw you man. I make him look that bad? He **is** that bad!"

We both changed the subject and soon after I realized that Derrick didn't care for me or took what I said seriously. Furthermore, I was truly done with all his bullshit and this time for good.

I called to wish my nephew Nick Happy 13th Birthday, I also had to talk with Pauli. She told me that Marla and Nessa were also there. I found out that Pauli and her younger sister were now talking to each other again. Pauli asked if I wanted to talk to Marla and I said I would but I was very nervous while I waited for Marla to come to the phone. I hadn't spoken to Marla in eight years. But it seemed that

I was nervous for no reason. Our conversation went smoothly and easily between us as if we hadn't missed any time at all. Marla and I rekindled our friendship and were as close as before as another piece of the puzzle fell into place.

As 2005 began, early in the year Ellen and Trey were moving away so we arranged a going-away party. It was a great party with both familiar and unfamiliar faces. That night I got a lot of attention from both people I know and didn't know. I enjoyed every compliment I got, absorbed them like a sponge. However, I drank too much and the day after I felt like crap. Not only did I have the worst hangover, I was beating myself up for drinking so much. I looked at myself in the mirror, *'Hannah, stop beating yourself up. Yes, you drank too much but there is nothing you can do about it now, so just get over it.'*

I started to reflect on my life and I realized that, I am the only one who can make changes in my life and I deserved something much better. I had promised Ellen to help clean the apartment, so I put some clothes on and walked down the few blocks to Ellen's apartment where I'd parked my car the night before. The other girls were already there. We all helped with the packing and moving, finishing up everything in the apartment before it would be time for Ellen and Trey to leave. As I walked from the apartment complex, I hear someone say, "Hey girl, what's your name?"

I turn my head towards a car parked in the middle of the street. A young Black man had rolled down his car window. I smiled.

"Hannah. Why?"

"Come here for a minute, let me talk to you."

I walked down the stairs and over to where he was parked. He was charming,

"I bet you are not aware of how incredibly beautiful you are, and your smile...oh my God. I'm Terence by the way."

I looked down into the grass as he continued,

"Do you have a boyfriend?" Now I looked up and our eyes met,

"No I don't, and thank you."

"How come you don't have a boyfriend? You *know* how beautiful you are with those eyes. I bet you looked in the mirror this morning when you woke up and said, 'damn girl you are fine.' I couldn't help myself but I started to laugh,

"Yeah right. The reason I don't have a boyfriend is I haven't met anyone good enough for me."

Since I came to the US I had lost 60 lbs, but it seemed like my mind couldn't see what I saw in the mirror every morning. From time to time, I looked at myself saying, *nothing changed*. It was time for me to go back in, but before Terence drove off, he gave me his phone number. When I returned to the apartment I had a broad smile on my face. Patricia asked me

"What was up with you?" so I told her.

"Guy's, guy's, guy's. We can't live with them and we can't live without them.
Life is funny girl. I just dumped D and the next minute, a stranger gives me his phone number."

We both laughed and finished up with the apartment.

Visitor from Sweden

I was summer 2005. My mother was still talking to Millay, my brother's ex girlfriend who asked if she could come to visit me.

"I would love for you to come visit with me," I said.

Mom is the only one who has visited me. To have my friend come visit would be awesome. Millay and I planned that she would visit in April 2006 and stay for a month. Millay's visit would be the same time that Mimi and Jeff would be married in Las Vegas, a perfect time and place. That was our weekend in Vegas and Chrystal came with us also. The three of us had a blast!

I was very happy I went to Mimi and Jeff's wedding. It was extremely emotionally and incredibly beautiful. Mimi reminded me of a Barbie doll and she had such a glow in her eyes. She was happy and Jeff was truly her soul-mate. I was genuinely happy for them. Patricia who now lived in Dallas, Mimi and I were not as close as we were before. Distance does that to a friendship. We all had our own life but we would still always remain friends.

While Millay was here the month passed by so quickly, we shopped, partied and I took her to many of the tourist places. She noticed how much I had grown as a person and that I was in control of my life and it showed. I put my foot down, a position that my friends from Sweden had never seen in me and they were surprised to see. I felt great about it. '*Well done Hannah.*'

OK it was time for Millay to leave, time for us to say goodbye. I missed the company at first and my apartment felt lonely, but a few days later, I was back to my normal routine.

I never been interested in on-line dating but now I thought, *why not try it?* So I signed up for Match.com. A short time later, I was on my way to give online dating a try. Alec was the first man who responded. Alec was a year older than me, he had a daughter who lived with her mother on the East Coast; he worked at Children's Hospital in the credentialing office. He also worked as an extra in the "industry" as a model/actor, so he said. He was easy to talk to; we talked for an hour and a half the first time we spoke. I was excited to meet him. We met a few days later. He was tall, 6 foot 2 and good looking. Alec was not just a good-looking man, we had great conversation as well. In the beginning, I was very skeptical but Alec surprised me by always calling when he said he would. He followed through when we made plans. One night on my way home from Tony's house my phone rang and it was Alec. I was surprised because it was 1:15 a.m. in the early morning, Alec said,

"Hannah, are you at home?"

"No I'm down the street from my house. Why?"

"Can I come over? I was out with my boys when I suddenly thought; 'damn I miss her.'"

I smiled for myself,
"Yes Alec you can come over. I'll meet you at the house. I'll be home in five minutes."

When Alec arrived to my house and put his arms around me, the way he squeezed me, told me how much he had missed me. I slowly started to trust Alec more and more. Alecs' roommate, Levy, never had a problem when I visited their house. Alec and Levy were out clubbing almost every night, and he explained that,

'When you're in the industry, you need to be out networking all the time.'

It made sense to me and I would never try to control Alec by telling him to stop doing what he was doing. I remembered all those years with Jared. How he controlled everything in my life, whom I was seeing, when or if I was allowed to see whoever. Where I was going and when it was time to do whatever. I wouldn't wish that on anyone!

After Alec and I had been dating for a couple of months, Levy couldn't afford his life style anymore, with the car note and rent, so he was going to move back to San Diego. That meant Alec would have to find another place to live but it wouldn't be easy and the deposit would be high as Alec's credit was bad so. Without thinking it through and being the unselfish person that I am, I said,

"You can stay with me for two to three months, if you want. It will give you a chance to save up the deposit quicker if you don't have to pay rent."

We both were aware that this arrangement was only for a few months. Alec wanted to make sure that it was without any boyfriend/girlfriend commitment.

"I'm trying to help you, not frame you Alec." I continued, "You need to understand one thing, and that even though I like you and enjoy being with you that doesn't mean that I can't live without you. I had a life before you and will have a life after you, so don't even think that; okay?"

Alec did not have a car or a cell phone. For whatever reason he said, but that wasn't an issue for me. But if you like someone, I believe you build together.

However, only a few weeks later together we got Alec a car, a used Lexus GS 300. I did the negotiating, because Alec is too stubborn for his own good. I helped him by making the down payment, which Alec gave me back most of that money. I also gave him the other cell phone on my account because I did not feel comfortable with him being out on the streets without a cell phone. What if there is an emergency? *All my "what if's."*

"Just for emergency," Alec said when I gave him the cell phone.

One night when Alec got home after been out clubbing, he woke me up and I could hear that he was drunk. He told me how happy he was for his car and thanked me so much for helping him get it.

"I love you for that,"

One thing what I noticed with him, was that Alec was afraid of 'losing' control of his emotions and always had his guard up. When Alec was sober, he never talked about feelings, but when he had had one too many drinks, that's when he spoke from the heart. Alec went out with his boys, but most of the time he came home at night, unless he was in another city. Sometimes one or more of his friends slept here on the couch or mattress on the floor in the living room. I could see that Alec became more and more comfortable with me. Even though he had told me that the cell phone was just for emergencies, more and more people started to call him on that phone. When the phone bill came, I asked him for money which he sometimes would give me. I still didn't ask him for money for the rent. I let Alec live with me so he could save money.

I realized that Alec did not put much effort into looking for an apartment and he didn't even try to save his money. He got paid on Friday, and the following Monday, most of his money was already gone. So he was always asking me for a $10 or $20 for gas or something. A few months went by and Alec hadn't found a place. I don't even know if he was looking for one. Alec willingly drank the alcohol and ate everything in the house, but he never bought anything back to replace what he finished. When I questioned something, Alec always had excuses. He was full of excuses.

I know I was the one that offered to help but I should have stopped this situation long time ago. I just care too much. I had a horrible feeling of guilt imagining that Alec wouldn't have any place to rest his head if I kicked him out. So I just shut up and tried to figure out how to handle it. Alec's family lived in Kansas City and even though he had a lot of other friends, most of them were more like "hang out" friends.

Not the kind of people Alec could depend on. I know I am that type of friend, so I was hoping that maybe Alec would realize that he needed to get his life together and take it more seriously. Alec was full of talk, plenty of talking, but no action! His plans sounded great, but there was no follow up on the plans. It was frustrating. I had been in this country for only a few years and I had my life under control and that without a social security number. I just could not understand.

I've met nice guys that would have been great men and wonderful boyfriends or husbands, but if they can't get themselves together I can't get involved in a relationship. I liked Alec because it seemed that he was together at least he talked that way and I believed him. But now when he lived with me and I could see the full picture it was different. Alec was too comfortable in this situation. He was not making any effort to get himself together; well no effort that I saw. So I regret that I offered him a place to live because now he was taking me for granted. I deserve better. I think Alec was so comfortable and perhaps thought that I needed him and so at this point it was safe for him to be his true self. He used to always answer the phone when I called. Now he didn't. We made plans and he was a no show. When I asked that he repay me whatever he borrowed or for bills, he didn't. He let me down on many occasions. I was getting upset too often and Alec was the cause.

All my life there has never been anyone I could count on. But I cannot accept a promise without the delivery. I get very upset and disappointed and it causes me to want to stop communicating with whoever made the promise. I know this seems weird and that it is as a result of issues from my past. I don't usually make plans; I prefer to play it by ear and go with the flow, unless it is with someone I know I can trust. Alec promised to come to my birthday celebration at a downtown restaurant. I was looking forward to introducing him to my friends. Well Alec never showed up and he didn't even call. I was very angry and upset. If I couldn't count on him when it was important to me, why should I trust him at all? This was my childhood being played all over again when I got hurt over and over again. So I confronted him. But he had some lame excuse as usual. I knew Alec was out partying and drinking and I always worried that something may have happened to him. He knew the circumstances of Mark's death and how difficult it was for me during that time. I was not fully over that trauma and I thought Alec would be more considerate of my feelings and call to let me know that he was okay. When I asked him why he didn't call me, he said

"I don't have to respond to anyone."

Basically, Alec didn't give me the respect I deserved. We were arguing more and more about everything and he would blame whatever on me. Each time, I got a little more hurt and my guard was up as soon as there was some discussion. I finally had had enough. It was time for him to move out. Our constant arguing got me more and more upset, and the fact that Alec was not contributing to the house and living off me. It seems he had stopped looking for an apartment because he was quite comfortable here. He had lodging and food and everything else he needed. He was too comfortable. I was not.

One day I told him it was time for him to move out as neither of us needed this constant stress. He moved out and in with another woman. I called him a month later and told him that I was going to turn off his cell phone. He begged me to keep it on until he got back home from the hospital. I didn't know Alec was in the hospital.

I felt sorry for him. He told me he had hurt his knee while playing basketball and would need surgery soon.

"This phone is the only way my mom and family can reach me and I need them now," Alec said.

Understandable and I felt bad for him. He knew which of my strings to pull. I said okay, but only until he felt better and got the surgery done. He had the surgery and then he started calling me a few times a week. Now we were actually talking without arguing. He complained about where he was living; he complained that the woman tried to tie him up, and that he didn't care for her like that and that it was too much drama for him. Now he was realizing how great he had it when he lived with me.

We hadn't seen each other in some time, so we arranged to meet for lunch. This was right after his surgery when he came home from the hospital and on crutches. I felt sorry for him and to see him like that, kind of weak and seemingly helpless. I tried to steel myself and tried not to care, but I did. At lunch, we talked and Alec asked if he could move back in for a short time. I made the mistake again and I said it would be okay. The arrangement this time would be only as friends where he slept in the living room. I was getting over my feelings for him but I still wasn't dating anyone.

In the beginning all was going well, perhaps because Alec was much calmer than I'd seen him before. But after he was feeling better and his leg was healing nicely, he was quickly getting back to his old ways and habits as when he first lived at my home. I started to feel more and more as if my house was no longer mine. Every evening as I drove home I would get this queasy feeling in my stomach. As I drove down the driveway to my home I was hoping that Alec's car would not be there. I was beginning to dread going home and often thought, *'I wish Alec would get the hell out so I could get my home back.'*

One day while we were chatting, I asked Alec if he had found an apartment. He shuffled in the chair seemingly uncomfortable by my question,

"No. I can't reach my friend who was going to cosign for me."

"Alec, let me ask you a question, do you want me to see if I can find an apartment for you and I will cosign the papers?"

"But you don't even have a social security number, so how could you?"

"I can somehow…. or at least I can try. Do you want me to try or not?"

"Yes if you can, let us try."

I had been thinking about it for a while. I knew it was not in my best interest, but I had had enough. I couldn't have him living with me any longer. I was too unhappy. I did not have a life on my own and figured this was my only way out. Alec had to get out. I desperately needed Alec to move because he was causing me too much stress. I started to feel as if I was suffocating when Alec was home. I needed him out before I had a nervous breakdown. This was a desperate situation and I was desperate. I needed my space back, so I could be at ease and in peace. Alec didn't consider my feelings, it was all about him. He was too selfish and too sure that I couldn't live without him and so he would treat me however he pleased.

It took me only eight days. The apartment manager showed me an apartment and we signed the lease. I was very happy and I again proved to myself that I can maneuver and do whatever it takes to survive. We told Barbara, the landlord, that I was the one moving in and that Alec was my boyfriend, so that she would see him around a lot. I started the countdown, and couldn't wait for Alec to move out.

Friday Alec was to have the remainder of the rest and last part of the rent money. The last thing I remember telling him was to leave the money at home and not take it with him that night. Why would he listen to me? When I got home from work, Alec was already home and gone out. I tried to reach him that Friday night but there was no answer. I left him a reminder of our meeting with Barbara and that he should call me back. No respond. Saturday morning came but Alec was a no show. I had a bad feeling in my body that something was going to go wrong, but I hoped not this time. I just couldn't take anymore. Alec was living in my house and not carrying his weight and not paying for anything.

I couldn't trust him to be here if I ever needed him. I kept calling Alec, but his cell phone was off. He was going to let this deal fall through and I felt as if he stayed away purposely. Now he would have a reason not to move. *'No, that can't happen, it just can't.'* How can I get rid of this feeling of desperation? I texted Tammy, she's one of the security women at work. I was so upset and I kept thinking *'what if?'* But there is no "*what if*", I can't take another "*what if*". Alec has to go, that was the only solution. After Tammy and I texted back and forth a few times, she called me.

"Hannah, don't talk to him today. You are upset now, so wait."
"I can't T. Alec knew damn well what was going on, that he had to sign the lease and pay the rent, and now his phone is turned off. He has pushed me too far this time T. If he wants to fuck with me, I am going to show him who he is fucking with. I don't care if he gets the apartment now. He's got to go!"

I was in a panic thinking of him being in my house longer. Barbara at the apartment had called me twice but I didn't answer her call as I didn't know what to say. She would have heard my voice and know something was wrong. Around 7:00 p.m., I heard the key in the door. It was Alec coming in as if all was well. The only thing he had time to do was sit down on a chair before I asked him if he was happy now that he had lost the apartment. I was standing on the other side of the table from him, asking,

"Why did you have to fuck this up? Why didn't you have your phone on so this could go smoothly?"

Alec just looked at me and said, "First, there is something wrong with my phone, and, second it's not your business where I was."

"No maybe it's not, but it is my business that you're still in my apartment and I don't want you here."

"Well I'm not leaving, so what are you going to do now?"

He looked up at me with arrogance written all over his face. He wanted me to back off. I picked up the phone and called Leon, a CHP officer, but he didn't answer so I left a message. I asked him to call me back. Alec was dialing his phone and he said,
"You think you can mess with me like that, bitch? I'll show you. I'm calling the Immigration on you and get you kicked out from this country. Hello, can I have the number for Immigration?"

I just stood there looking at him. I couldn't believe what I had just heard. After all I had done for this man, and he was now calling Immigration on me. This is unbelievable! Without a word to me, just a "thank you" to the operator, Alec hung up and dialed another number. I was about to grab his phone but he put it away and snapped mine right out of my hand and threw it at the wall and it broke into pieces.

"Now who you going to call, huh?"

I started to get a very uncomfortable. A feeling I knew all too well. I was being pushed into a corner and my survival instinct was aroused. Alec got up and moved over to the couch where he laid back on the armrest and turned the TV on. *'He needs to get out,'* kept replaying in my mind. *'Before things get worse he needs to get out.'* With the calmest of voice I said,

"I want you to leave Alec. Now."

Alec looked over at me with a look of contempt,

"I am not going anywhere."

I bent down and turned off the TV manually. He turned it back on with the remote. I sat down on the mattress on the floor next to the entertainment center, this is where Alec had been sleeping and I turned off the TV again. He got up, kicked the glass top table off its legs and it landed next to me, half on the floor and half on the mattress. Then he sat down and turned the TV back on with the remote. He must have used all his strength to have that glass top table move that far because that was a heavy table. *'I can't do this anymore. I can't do this again!! I need to get him out from here before things get more serious.'*

I leaned forward and put my hand on the TV power cord by the outlet and Alec jumped up from the couch again. He hissed between his teeth with something of a threat,

"I wish you would. I'll break your fucking table."

Alec put his foot in the middle of the glass top table. I looked him straight in the eyes and pulled the cord out. He stamped on the tabletop and the glass broke in a hundred pieces. As Alec walked by me, he raised his hand only a few inches from my face and hissed, "Bitch."

He never touched me but now he had shown me that he would not hesitate to hit me. I would never trust him again. *NEVER. 'I can't even call the police. What if they come here, and take me in when Alec tells them I'm in the country illegally?'*

Without a word, I got up from the floor and picked up my old cell phone, a flip phone. Alec snapped it from my hand and bent the top off and started to walk back towards the couch. I walked through the kitchen towards the door. As soon as I reached the door and Alec understood I was about to leave, he came running. He pulled me away from the door and into the bedroom. At this point, I just wanted to get away. It had already gone too far. I started to twist and turn, trying to twist myself out of his grasp, but he used his weight to restrain me and he was too strong for me to get away. He held me in that grasp until I calmed down. I knew all too well that in a situation like that, I was vulnerable.

It was late and I fell into a restless sleep, I was emotionally exhausted and Alec was too. I woke up, still lying under Alec. I moved and it woke him up. Now that I was calmer I had to think clear and smart, for my own safety. I was emotionally tired, tired of fighting and tired of arguing about nothing. I was so tired of "he said and she said" with arguments without any solutions. Alec never admitted that he was wrong. He never apologized so it was pointless. I called my job from his phone and told them I'd be late because of some personal issues. I got in the shower and suddenly my whole body started to shiver and I started to cry.

I thought about what had happened and I became conscious of how Alec had violated me and my house. He knew damn well that I had been to hell and back to get here and achieve what I had. But Alec still did not hesitate to disrespect me and violate my space. When he broke my table and my phones, he broke parts of me. There are only things but I worked hard to get them.

Besides, Alec had used what he knew was my weak spot, he had called Immigration. I couldn't understand how Alec had the heart to be so mean after all the help I been to him. That is what I get for trying to be a good friend, and woman who put her cards on the table, a friend that will be there in good and bad times to help the best I can. Alec took my kindness for weakness and that was his mistake. I got out of the shower and wrapped a towel around me when Alec came into

155

the bathroom. When he saw me shivering and crying, he caressed me, saying more to himself than to me,

"We'll work this out, right? We have to work this out."

I did not answer I just got dressed and was about to clean up all the glass in the living room, but Alec said he'd take care of it.

"I promise you Hannah that I will compensate you for the two cell phones, table top and wine glasses I broke."

I was emotionally spent plus I didn't believe a word of what he said, so I told him,

"Alec, I only have one question for you and it is just a yes or no answer, okay?"

"Sure, what's up?"

"Do you want the apartment or not?"

"Yes."

"I didn't call Barbara yesterday and I'm not sure she will still rent it to me, but I can call and see what she says."

After last night, Alec had to go now. I got a new phone and when I got to work, I called Barbara, excused myself for yesterday and said I still wanted the apartment. I asked her to please give me another chance. She wasn't too happy but said okay, just because she likes me I could still have the apartment. I called Alec and gave him the news and a week later, he moved into his own place. It was fantastic to be by myself again. Finally, that uneasiness feeling in my stomach disappeared and I felt free again.

I couldn't help asking myself, *'why am I always looking for validation from the wrong men? I declared I wanted a relationship with a definition, and then I turn around and am attracted to men who won't give it to me. They don't want to be called my man, but we are more than friends. I am attracted to men who do not want to commit, but they didn't want anyone else to have me, and it should be on their terms and when and how they wanted. I was always open from the beginning; I told them how I am. I am very emotionally, I show affection, say what's on my mind, good and bad. I am sensitive, especially when it comes to certain things. I want someone I can trust, communicate with, and someone I know will be there to catch me and pull me up when I am weak. I don't mind if they want their space to hang out with their friends, their "boys", as long as they are telling me and I know that they want to be with me. I need them to reassure me that they like me. If they don't, I start to feel insecure. If I assume that they have feelings for me, sooner or later, it seems like it comes back to bite me in the ass. I mention something that was not suitably for them and their pride got in our way. No compromising. It was their way or no way.'*

Marla's visiting

Marla called me and said she wanted to come visit me. I hadn't seen her in 10 years so I couldn't wait to meet her again. We had a lot of catching up to do. February 12, 2007, the day after my birthday, I headed for LAX to pick up Marla. I parked the car and went to the waiting area. I was so nervous I didn't know what to do. I got coffee at Starbucks to keep my hands busy for the time being. I bought a little teddy bear to give to Marla. As I waited I squeezed him and held him tightly against my chest. People must have thought I was high on something because I just could not stand still. The only thing I was high on, was happiness that I finally would have a chance to see my "little sister" again after ten, long years. And now Marla would have a chance to see my new life, and how happy I was. Something she's never seen before. My adrenaline was pumping and I started to have a little difficulty breathing from excitement. I recognized her right away and ran to caress her, crying with happiness. When we got to the house and Marla started to unpack we talked about this and that, just running off at the mouth. The subject turned to our past, about Jared and the last time Marla and I talked.

"I have something with me and I believe it's yours Hannah."

"Something that is mine? What is it?"

I was so excited. Marla unwrapped something from the suitcase and I couldn't believe my eyes when I saw what it was. It was the blue antique vase that I got from my grandmother. The vase was the only thing I had from big mama.

"How did you get that? When I left…..I couldn't get anything, so how?"

"Do you remember when Pauli and Ron helped Jared to clean out the apartment after you left, because he couldn't have anything that reminded him of you, Pauli found this and thought it was yours, so she saved it for you."

I remembered and got lost in my thoughts for a second as I thought of when Pauli had told me about that. Jared had asked Pauli and Ron to clean out my things from the apartment--curtains, bed sheets, towels etc., everything that reminded Jared of me. I understood it was his way of moving on so he could "forget" me. While Pauli and Ron had been in the apartment, cleaning out, she put away some of the things that Pauli knew were mine, without telling Jared. She thought I deserved to have my things and she had sent me a package 2004 with some of my journals and books of poems from years back. Now Marla came with my blue vase. I couldn't thank her enough for being so considerate and thinking of me.

"Hannah, you know I never stopped thinking of you as my sister. I just didn't want to have anything to do with Jared. When Pauli told me that you had left my brother, I laughed out loud and thought, *YES she did it, at last!*"

"You know I would not be alive today if I haven't left."

"Oh I know. Honestly, I never thought you would get out of it alive. I never thought you would leave him."

"Come on girl, you know me. I do whatever I have to, to survive" as I winked at her.

"What matters is that you did leave him before he killed you Hannah."

"Yes you are right. And I am so happy that you and I have connected again. I missed you so much."

"I missed you too."

I gave Marla another hug, we began catching up on all those years we missed. She told me how things were going with my niece and nephews. For that week of Marla's visit, we could not stop talking. We had so much to say and the time was short. But we had an outstanding week. We went shopping every day and drove around the whole Los Angeles.

On February 17, Marla, I and some friends had my belated birthday get together and it was great. I had invited a few friends, and others came with my friends. But the best part was that Marla was here to celebrate it with me. But as you know, everything comes to an end and Marla had to go back to Sweden. Marla and I promised each other that it would definitely not take another ten years before we saw each other again. I waited at the airport and watched her walk away until I could not see her any longer. And I once again was leaving the airport with emptiness in my heart as another loved one left. But life has to go on.

Just after Marla returned to Sweden, Pauli and Marla had another disagreement and stop talking to each other again. As they are like my sisters, they both communicate with me, so I told them that I would be happy to listen to them vent, but that I was not going to take sides. It is there fight, what is between them is between the two of them.

Met someone who'd change my life

It was mid-January, Chrystal, Katie, and I decided to have a girls' night out and go to a club up in Hollywood. Chrystal and I got to the club as the arranged time, but Katie, who I met through one of my Swedish girlfriends, would be late as always. Vince, a guy I've known since 2001, was a promoter of this club and had given me a hookup contact I should talk to when we got to the club. My girlfriends always let me do the talking, as I can talk to anyone very easily. I went to the front of the line and I was just about to speak when a young man next to me tapped my arm. When I turned around, he whispered in my ear,

"Ask for Brock, he'll let you girls in." I smiled and winked at him, then whispered back,

"Thanks."

Brock was the same name that Vince had given me and he had described him as tall and about 6'4". He was playing difficult at first and questioned why he should let us in before the others in line.

"Because I know Vince and you are such a nice guy, that is why."

I smiled a broad smile and flashed my deep blue eyes at him. Again, he pretended to be serious, but behind that look, I could see his eyes were smiling.

"Excuse me." Another guy came up behind me and told Brock, "Hey B, let the two blondes in. They are with me."

He gentle laid his hand on my lower back and escorted us in. I turned my head to see who my "black knight" was, and my eyes met the biggest and most beautiful smile I had seen in a long time. He was a handsome Black man, slender, taller than me but shorter then Brock, and I believed he was a manager, promoter or something. It seemed like he knew everyone there. Brock put a VIP band on both our wrists, Chrystal and mine, and he promised we would see him later. He then wished us a nice evening. The man with the beautiful smile led me to the stairs. I put my head to the side, looking up at him with one of my big smiles.

"Thank you. That was very nice. What is your name?" He was still holding his arm around my waist and he took my hand with his other hand,

"No problem. Vince is my boy and I heard you mention his name for Brock so I thought I'd help you out. My name is Devin. Yours?"

I got up one stair so we were standing face to face, and even though his hand was no longer on my waist, I could still feel the warmth of his palm still lingered at my waist.

"I'm Hannah, nice to meet you Devin. And thank you again."

"My pleasure Hannah. Enjoy your evening and I'll catch you later."

"Sure."

I grabbed Chrystal's hand and we went to the bar to get a drink before we sat down on the patio so she could smoke. She got an apple martini while I ordered a Raspberry vodka with 7-up.

"That was so nice of him," Chrystal said.

"And he was so handsome too," I replied.

Then I looked down, suddenly remembered his eyes and looked at Chrystal from the corner of my eye, saying almost more to myself then to her.

"He had the most genuine eyes I've seen since Mark." I shook my head as if to shake my memories away, thinking *'is it ever going to stop hurting thinking of what happened to Mark?'*

We went up to the VIP area and as the night worn on, the club got more crowded. The young guy who told me about Brock came and danced with me for a little bit and as soon as I sat down again, I saw someone walking towards me. He looked familiar and when he came closer, I saw it was Devin.

"Hey, I heard you girls were rocking the floor."

Katie had showed up by now but both she and Chrystal were dancing so Devin sat down next to me,

"Hannah, I have a meeting to go to, so I came to make sure everything is good with you before I leave."

"Everything is just great. I'm getting a little tired but we are having a great time."

Again, he put his arm around my back as he got a little closer and said,

"I would love to see you again. Can I get your number?"

I was debating with myself for a second before I answered him. *'He is nice, handsome and everything, but maybe he just a player, he seems too comfortable and knew all the right things to say.'* I had been burned so much through my life and lately, and it seemed like I always attracted the wrong men. I wanted to buy myself some time without losing him.
"How about it if I got yours and I'll call you?"

"Oh so you can put it in the trash as soon as I'm gone?" Devin said seriously.

"If I wasn't going to call you, I wouldn't ask for the number." Now it was my turn to look serious.

It was time for him to leave and we both stood up. For a second, his brown eyes just looked straight into my blue eyes before he pulled me closer. As he did, all my senses woke up and a pleasant shiver went through my whole body. The attraction was obvious.

"Bye Hannah. I'm looking forward to talking with you soon again."

I could hardly speak after the feeling his touch just woke up in me, so I just smiled and said,

"Yeah we'll talk soon. Bye Devin and good luck with your meeting."

The following days I couldn't stop thinking about Devin. What Alec had done was still fresh in my memory and I was hurt and scared. Not because Alec wouldn't admit that he had feelings for me, but the way he had violated my house, breaking my things, and called Immigration when we had that last fight, when he refused to leave when I asked him to.

I had promised to call Devin, so one day when my job was slow I dialed his number. No answer so I left a message with my phone number when it went to his voicemail. Only a minute later my phone rang and it was Devin returning my call.

"Hey what's up Hannah?"

"Nothing much, just working," I smiled. "So you don't answer private numbers huh?"

"No most of the time I don't, but when I heard it was you, I had to call you back."

"See, I told you I would call."

"I know. I have to tell you Hannah. I love your voice with that accent. You sound so beautiful and sweet."

"Thanks, but I've been trying to shake my accent, but it doesn't work," I said and laughed.

"No Hannah. Keep it. I love it."

We talked for a few minutes, wished each other a great day and we would talk later. Devin was saying all the right things and seemed to be a big flirt, but he also seemed to be genuine. I was happy that I had called him and I couldn't get him out of my mind for the rest of that day. We continued to call each other almost every day and talked about getting together. I realized Devin was a very busy man, and it just didn't seem we could get our schedules coordinated and find a time to meet. I was working all day and he was working mostly graveyard shift. He called a few times later in the evening, asking if he could come over to my house, but I said no. Not yet, he scared me. Not him personally, but the attraction was already strong between us, I thought. I missed skin touching skin, my back against a man's muscular chest and arms wrapped around my shoulders, hands reaching out to take mine and that's how we'd fell asleep. I was coming to the realization that if I didn't respect myself, I would never find a man who respected me.

I felt like what Devin and I had between us, was something real. I didn't want to ruin whatever that feeling might be, by having sex with him and then find out that that was all he wanted. Been there and done that. Or even worse, make love to Devin and fall in love with him. That could be wonderful if it was mutual, but what if it was just me falling for him? I would rather keep Devin only as a friend, than to lose him because sex complicates things, sex often grows feelings. I don't know how much more hurt and disappointment I could take. I really don't want to be scared and being afraid to fall in love with someone again. Well, maybe I am not really scared to love someone, but I am afraid that "that" someone wouldn't love me. That no one could love me, as I have heard for all those years with Jared. Besides, the other men I met had never said they love me, so I have these doubts.

I fell in love with Mark and he died. I had started to believe that Alec loved me and lowered my guard to let go of my fears and he violated my house. I realized that Alec wouldn't let go of his pride and ego which was his fear, I think.

Devin and I went on a date and had a great time. When it was time to go our separate ways, Devin escorted me to my car. I unlocked the door and turned around to thank him for the evening. He was standing right behind me. He put his arms around my shoulders and pulled me close to him. I could feel his heart beat and after a few seconds, I looked up at him smiling and he placed a feather soft kiss on my lips.

The next time Dev asked if he could come over and see me I was in agreement. It was a Friday I remember, and I had just come home from the gym. I was watching "MTV Cribs" on television when Devin arrived. All we did was sitting on the couch and talk. He stayed a while and then left for work. When we said goodbye at the door, Devin leaned forward and gave me a kiss and quickly left. I got in the shower and could still feel the touch of his lips against mine. There was something with Devin that scared me and at the same time it attracted me. *'What is this man doing to me?'* but yet I couldn't put my finger on what it was.

Devin and I started to see each other a few times per week and the feeling I've had from that very first moment we met got stronger, I mean regarding his eyes. He was genuine and since I had started to date Devin, when my nightmares came I could control them, they didn't control me. My dreams didn't have me waking up from panic attacks anymore. I thought about the saying "be careful what you wish for", and Devin was that kind of man I'd been wishing for. Someone I could count on to be there when I needed him. That scared the hell out of me, as I had only had that once before in my life and that was with Mark. I promised myself to do whatever it takes to get over my fear.

That was easier said than done. One night Devin called me and asked if he could come over, and of course, I said yes. He never showed up and when I tried to call him, there was no answer. The fear I felt when I had lost Mark swept over me. I started to sweat. My breathing got faster and my eyes filled with tears. *'Stop Hannah, nothing has happened,'* I tried to convince myself, but it didn't help. I was close to panicking and the chatterbox in my head was taking over, thinking "what if this and what if that." Devin had never before said he was on his way and then never showed up. Why did he have to do that now? I left a voice message, asking him to call me as soon as possible just to let me know he was okay. I fell back in a restless sleep and when I woke up early the next morning, there was still no phone call or text message from Devin.

Jane called me around noon to invite me over the night to watch a UFC fight on cable and I accepted. Ellen's boyfriend Trey had introduced Jane and her husband Patrick to me at SWEA's yearly Christmas fair a few years ago, our friendship grew stronger, and they are now two of my best friends. I needed to get my focus on something else and accepted Jane's invitation. Around 3:00 p.m. Devin returned my call.

"I got your message Hannah. What's up? I fell asleep." He said as it was the most common thing in the world, but I had made a decision, I had to leave Devin alone. I didn't blame Devin for it, but from the way I was reacting, I knew that I had started to develop strong feelings for him. I had to prevent my feelings from growing stronger. I couldn't let myself to get so attached. I was already more attached than I wanted to be and I wasn't sure how to handle the situation or how he felt for me.

That evening I went over to Jane's to watch the UFC fight. I picked Shannon up, she is the housekeeper at The Ashers and she had become a wonderful friend. When we got there, three other people were already there. I introduced myself to Richard and his girlfriend Tamika, and this good-looking younger man Tyrese. Our conversation flowed easily but unfortunately, the fight turned out to be extremely short. One fighter was knocked out in the first ten minutes. The rest of the evening passed by fast and we had a great time. Richard and Tamika left first and when we were ready to leave, Tyrese left too. After saying goodbye to Jane and Patrick, we thanked them for a wonderful evening, Tyrese walked Shannon and me to the car to made sure we were safe. I unlocked the car, turned around and gave him a hug and with a mischievous smile I said,

"Thank you Tyrese. It was very nice to meet you."

"My pleasure, Hannah. Drive safe, okay?"

He didn't ask for my phone number and I wasn't going to ask. If this had happened before I met Devin, I would've asked Tyrese for his number without any hesitation. But I had promised myself not to do things like that anymore and only date one man at the time. Dating more than one person at the time makes it difficult to focus on the important things in that person.

A few days later when I went to Target with Shannon, my cell phone rang and even though I didn't recognized the number, I answered. To my surprise it was Patrick calling.

"Hey Hannah what's going on?"

"Nothing much. How is life with you and your family?"

"Oh it is great. Jane is in Las Vegas for work and little Peter is sleeping."
I smiled thinking of how big Peter was getting …

"Nice. So what's going on Patrick?"

"Do you remember Tyrese who was here the other night?"

"Oh yes, of course."
"Well I just spoke to him and he asked me to give you his phone number."

Now I laughed aloud, "Sure what it is?"

I was digging my hand in the purse to find a pen. Patrick gave me the number and after we hung up and I dropped Shannon at her house, I called Tyrese. He was on his way over to his father's house, but said he really wanted to see me again. So he cancelled the trip to his father to came over and visit me instead. None of the men I met after Mark had been big on showing affection. And I found that strange as I thought showing affection was an important part of any intimate relationship. Tyrese wasn't scared, and held my hand and hugged me. I realized how much I'd missed that affectionate interaction. I couldn't understand why I was attracting men who were afraid to commit and show affection when I am so willing to show my feelings.

Maybe I tried to play it safe. I thought it would be easier for me not to fall for them, as I knew they wouldn't give me what I wanted and then there would be a reason to kick them to the curb. I am told I love too much or too easily, but I don't think one can love too much. I personally think that some people just don't know how to receive love, or maybe was it me, but I don't think so.

I still saw Devin from time to time, not as often as before but it was hard for me to let him go. I'd thought maybe my feelings for Devin would calm down if I focused on Tyrese, but there was something about Devin. No one had ever made me so confused as Devin did. *'How can Dev have such an impact on me? I don't understand it.'*

It had only been a month since I first met Tyrese, when I realized that I had to make a decision. Although, I had been in the US for 8 years, I still could not get used to dating more than one person at a time without feeling guilty. I just didn't think it was right. There was no reason for me to feel that way, I wasn't committed to either Devin or Tyrese. But this wasn't about either of them, it was about me, and the how I felt. Guilt was a feeling I tried to avoid. I had to trust myself and do what was best for me. I thought about both men in my life and weighed the odds. If Tyrese was here and Devin called, I felt horrible and just wanted Tyrese to leave so I could call Devin back. However, I didn't feel as much guilt in the reverse. So it seemed the answer was obvious. There was only one man I wanted to be with, and that was Devin. I told Tyrese we could only be friends, and it seems that he didn't mind.

A few nights after I made that decision and told Tyrese, Devin called to see if he could stop by before going to work and I said of course. Because I had made that decision I was more comfortable with just thinking of Devin and the thought made me smile. Even though our lifestyles, Devin's and mine, were different and all my senses told me to forget about him, I just couldn't. On the surface, Devin was the biggest flirt I'd ever met, but still there was that little voice within, telling me to trust him, and I did. With his judgment, I would put my life in his hands before my parents. I know he would do what was best for me. Knowing that and against everything I'd believed in before, another very important answer came to me as I watched television with Devin. We were discussing our day-to-day life and when Devin was about to leave again I said,

"Hold on for a second. Can you do me a favor?"

"Sure, what's up H?"

"Can you hold on to these for me?"

I handed Devin something I was holding in my hand, he look down and with surprise in his voice he said,

"Your keys. Why?"

"For whatever you want. I might lock myself out you know. Or you might be hungry and I'm not home. Maybe you just want to surprise me."

I was happy I just had a few candles lit, because I was blushing as I mentioned the last thing. Devin said with a caring voice,

"No doubt sweetheart."

Sad news

If someone just could have warned me about how this day was going to go. I took a shower and I was already late so I was drinking my coffee while I was getting dressed. I also had to stop at the bank before I went to work. The woman teller I was talking to was really nice and we were chit-chatting a little while she was completing my transaction when my phone rang.

It was Marla and I heard right away something was wrong. Marla was crying and was speaking incoherently as she told me that her daughter Nessa and she were on their way to the hospital because she had just gotten a call from a doctor at the hospital. He told her that her mother Eileen came in there earlier by ambulance after she had a heart attack while she was downtown Gothenburg. The doctors had done all in they could for her, but unfortunately their efforts were without success. Eileen had passed away. I could hear Marla's pain and I too started to cry.

"Marla, how are you doing? I am so sorry. I wish I could be there for you now."

"Hannah I haven't talked to my mother in almost four years and never thought it would hurt so much."

"Hey girl, Eileen was still your mother so of course it hurts, and of course you will feel all kinds of confusing feelings."

I left the bank and got into my car to go to work. Pauli was at the hospital already, but the doctor told Marla that Jared hadn't arrived yet. Now Marla was worried that Jared would arrive while she was there. Marla's voice jolted me from the daze of my thoughts,

"Hannah I'm just walking into the hospital and I'll call you when we are leaving, ok? We need to keep our eyes open just in case Jared is in the bushes somewhere around here. You just can never know with him!"

"Okay, I understand and you know I'm here for you whenever, so call me back baby girl, and do me a favor and say goodbye to your mom from me too."

"Yeah I will, and thank you Hannah."

"Anytime sis. I love you."

I can't believe this is happening. I have known Eileen since I was fifteen years old, since I met Jared and now she's gone. What hurts the most is that I can't be there for Marla and Pauli. Both sisters hadn't spoken with one another for quite a while, and neither of them spoke to their psycho brother. Now the all three of them would have to get along. It's another nightmare starting all over again.

I went to Starbuck's to get a coffee and on the way to work my tears started to fall again. I was crying because I was frustrated. I was frustrated, because I knew that Marla and Pauli would have to see their brother again. I had told Marla that she should not to go to the funeral by herself but she didn't want anyone else to be involved in their family drama. I understood. It would be a risk for everyone who was involved with Marla, Pauli or me, if Jared found out who they were. They would become targets too by standing next to either of us. That is how that psycho's mind works! I thought up a solution for Marla, and called her back,

"You can always call the policeman, Ivar Back, the officer who came over to the women's shelter to talk to me about pressing charges against your brother, to see if he can do anything for you. Maybe he could get some protection for you by sending another policeman to go with you. I'll find his number for you when I get home."

Devin called to see how my day was going and it was almost like he had known something was wrong. I told him exactly what had happened and just the night before had told him about my situation with my ex Jared and how Marla and Pauli, his sisters, don't have contact or want contact with him, but both of them are my best friends. Devin was sympathetic to my story and he comforted me by saying,

"But Hannah, Marla knows you are with her even if you're not there. You're there in spirit baby." I know he was right.

I got to work but didn't get much done. I grabbed my mp3 player and took the dogs out for a walk with the hope that a brisk walk would help clear my mind. When I got back, I had a missed call from Pauli so I called her back. I expressed my sympathy and Pauli told me how it happened. Pauli had gone to the hospital as soon as they called her. The hospital had given her all her mother's belongings and Pauli said,

"Mom looked so peaceful as she was lying there in a white dress and flowers in her hands."

Eileen no longer had to stress over Jared and maybe for the first time in many years, had peace of mind. When Pauli spoke to the doctor about what had caused her death, the doctor said most likely it was a heart attack but they couldn't say until the autopsy. But to do the autopsy the doctors needed permission. Pauli thought about it for a minute and remembered how evil her brother is, and gave the doctors permission to go ahead with the autopsy. When Pauli told me I responded,

> "Well done. If nothing else, you would know Jared didn't have anything to do with your mother's death, and there would be no questions."

Eileen had been fairly young, only 65 years old. If Jared got the opportunity, he would start a living hell for both of his sisters. Pauli said that her mother had a lot of papers, money and other things people usually don't carry with them with her, things that one usually kept at home. That was confusing to Pauli and her family. Why would Eileen have all these things with her? Pauli, Ron and one of the sons went to Eileen's house to see if she had any animal or something that needed to be taken care of. Once at the house, Pauli had the answer why Eileen had all those papers with her and did not leave them at home. Jared and his family were living with Eileen at her place. He now had four kids with a young Estonian woman. Eileen probably had to support all five of them also. The Svenssons saw light in the apartment and rang the doorbell a few times but no one answered the door. When Pauli put the key in the lock, someone unlocked the top lock and opened the door. For the first time since Jared threatened Pauli's family, five years ago, she was now standing face to face with her brother.

> "Hannah you can't believe it. Jared hasn't changed a bit, absolutely nothing."

Pauli said and I honestly hadn't expected him to either.

> "The only difference was that Jared had gained some weight and it looked like he didn't take care of himself any more -- a few days' beard and his eyes were black. You know Hannah how he has that crazy "out of control" look?"

"Hey sis, you don't have to tell me. I already know all too well."

I could see Jared's face and the evilness in his eyes if I closed my eyes. It's amazing how clearly I still remember all this after eight years. I was also amazed when I realized what a difference between me now and when I first came to the US. Amazed at how much stronger I had grown, both mentally and personally, since I left Sweden and to hear that Jared is still the same. I always had an unpleasant shiver in my body, just hearing Jared's name, but not anymore. Then it hit me, *'Jared doesn't have any control over my mind anymore.'*

Back in Sweden, when the door opened Pauli and Ron took a step back and Jared said

"Oh, so it's time to come now, huh?" Those first words made them realize that Jared hadn't changed one bit.

"Hannah. I understood that Jared had never grown up. He was still the same person who needed to control everything as when he was a little boy. All these years I had thought he had changed, or would change, but now when I see that he hasn't, I understand how Jared manipulated my family and what a hell you must been living under."

Jared said he wanted their mother's belongings and Pauli had no right to anything after she had abandoned her mother for so long. Jared said,

"Now when our mother is dead, you think you can come and see what you can get from her."

Pauli did not bother to explain to Jared and she did not have to explain to me.

I already knew how Jared acts and how he thinks and I expect the worst from him. Now that Pauli knew there was no pet to rescue, they left. There was another kind of animal yes, but not one which could be saved! As Pauli and Ron started to walk down the stairs, Jared came down after them and locked the door from the outside. Probably so his wife and kids couldn't come outside while someone was there. Earlier, Marla had told me that Eileen told her how badly Jared was treating his children's mother, the same way he had treated me, and of course he controlled the whole family. Jared halted his steps when he saw that there was someone else around, a third person. He didn't know who the person was it could have been a police officer, so he played it safe. Better to be safe than sorry so he turned around and ran back into the house.

When Pauli, Ron and Jay got home, Nick told them that Jared had already called the house, and their youngest daughter, Wendy answered the phone. When Wendy asked who it was, Jared said Santa Claus. That was so typical of Jared, when Nick took the phone and asked who it was, Jared finally answered him. He called back again and talked to Pauli. First Jared spoke Finish with Pauli so Ron wouldn't understand if he was listening but Pauli kept answering him in Swedish, and so Jared switched to Swedish. He would do things like that when he had something fishy on his mind, or when he wanted to threaten someone and there wouldn't be any witnesses. The telephone call got disconnected and Pauli texted me back and said let's talk later.

The rest of the day was kind of crazy and I found it hard to concentrate. My knee was bothering me so I skipped my spinning and Pilates classes. I couldn't focus on anything anyway. I prayed before I went to bed and it was hard to fall asleep after all the events of the day. My mother, Patrick and I sent a flower arrangement to Eileen's funeral, to show our respect to Eileen and the daughters.

Another of Jared's attempt

One and a half years later, eighteen months, Jared decided to call my mother at 10 o'clock at night and ask for me. He said he just wanted to thank me for the flowers I had sent to his mother's funeral even though he didn't take the opportunity to thank my mother as well. That was only his excuse.

"Maybe if I give you my phone number, you can ask her to call me." He said. My mother actually wrote down his number. What a ......Why? After all things he had done to me and she learned he had done to me, my mother took his number. Unbelievable! I called Annie, my sister, and spoke to her and begged her to explain for our mother what price I had paid, and I was still paying to get out of that relationship alive. I even had to get a protected identity in Sweden; that is how serious my situation was, maybe still is. How could my mom be so disconnected. After all, she saw me at the hospital when I had just left Jared, with bumps and bruises, black and blue all over my body. How could mom even talk to him? Annie asked me not to be so hard on mom, that it is not that easy for her. Who the hell said that things are easy for me? I was so upset.

Found out the issue with my hip

My knee started to hurt more and more, just like when I was ten years old, and I got worried. I did my best to ignore the pain, I couldn't afford to go to the doctor as I didn't have any insurance. I told my boss about it with hopes that maybe they could do something for me. They are both doctors, and have connections. It took them two months before Martin and Judy finally spoke to Dr. Jordan for me. I explained my pain and the nurses took some x-rays of my knee and one of my hips. There it was, the same issue I had since I was a child, but even though it was properly diagnosed back then, my parents never bothered to fully understand when the doctor explained what the issue was all about. Dr. Jordan came in and showed me the x-ray of my hip.

"Hannah, you have something called Avascular necrosis of the femoral head."

"And what is that?"

Dr. Jordan explained that Avascular necrosis (AVN) of the femoral head is an increasingly common cause of musculoskeletal disability, and it poses a major diagnostic and therapeutic challenge. AVN represents a failure to supply adequate oxygen to underlying bone. Although patients are initially asymptomatic, AVN usually progresses to joint destruction, requiring total hip replacement, usually before the fifth decade. Dr. Jordan informed me in simple words, that the femoral head is supposed to be smoothly round, but with my disease, the femoral head has the shape of a cauliflower. That was why my hip makes snapping sounds at times. The reason the doctors had to put a screw in my hip at the age of ten, was that all my cells had been dead in the left side of my hip, and they had hoped that the screw would help to heal my hip and hopefully new cells would grow.

If my parents had asked questions as to why I needed a screw in my hip at that time, we would have known about this before. I would have had a chance to prevent the further damage. Dr. Jordan made it clear to me that I cannot jump, no running, no horseback riding. To simplify it, I should avoid pounding on my hip. That was how I could help my hip from further damage. I thanked Dr. Jordan and left for work. On my way there, I was thankful I had gone to the doctor. I'd never been a person who enjoy running, but after Mark's death, I took up running almost every day for a year. It was my way of trying to run away from the pain, from my sorrows and the anger. It was running that made me get rid of the "bad" energy of built up emotions, work out at the gym wasn't enough to reduce my anxiety. The only time I went running now, was when I did cardio at the gym. But now was the time for me to stop running, in more ways than one. I had to give myself peace.

Reunion after Eight years long years

While I was standing at the airport, waiting for Svensson's to come, I didn't know which foot I was going to stand on. *'How can I be so nervous when it's Pauli and my nephews? I haven't seen them in more than eight years and a lot has happened since then but anyway.'*

The passengers started to arrive, but I did not see Pauli and my nephews. I checked the time on my cell phone, it felt like I had been waiting forever, and the time was going so slowly and I remembered what Tim said when he was a little boy. We have a saying "when you're waiting for something good, you never wait too long" but Tim said "when you wait for something good, you always wait too long." That thought made me smile because that was exactly how I felt. I saw some young men who looked like them from afar, but when they came closer I realized I was mistaken. When I had been at the airport for about 90 minutes a young man came out with a cart and it took me a few seconds before I realized that it was Tim.

Oh my God how big he was. Then came Jay and Nick followed by their mother. When I saw Pauli, I was sure it was my nephews. The boys were so handsome and I thought my heart was going to explode with all the love I felt.

I walked towards them and the first one I hugged was Tim, who was such a fine looking young man now, and I felt my tears. Not a word by anyone, until I hugged Nick who was next. Nick was also a real cutie and a little clown when he said,

"You are so tiny. I remembered I always had to look up to you aunty."

"You still do Nick, in one way, at least."

The only one who had been taller than me when I last saw them was Jay, and now all three of them were way taller than I. It was Jay's turn to get a hug, he was probably as tall as his father, and even he was so handsome and as calm as could be. Last but not least, Pauli. She said it took so long to get through Customs because she had forgot that she had four tangerines in her pocket and Security had to write a report. I smiled,

"Welcome to Los Angeles."

We took all the suitcases and bags to the rental car I had, and luckily it was the perfect size for all of us and the bags. I took the streets back home as the rush hour had started and the freeway would be bumper to bumper. While we drove around the airport, I explained for them why we took the streets and Tim made me laugh when he said

"Oh, so you are telling me this is not the highway?"

177

"No it's not. The highways have at least four or five lanes and faster speed limit."

We stooped at Baja Fresh and ordered some take out before we finally headed to the house. I had put my other garage opener in the rental car and dropped them and the luggage off right outside the door to the stairs, before I parked. When I opened the door to the apartment I said, "Welcome home," and stepped aside so Jay, Tim, Nick and Pauli could come in. I knew they would take their shoes off in the hallway. They are Swedish. We had a house tour and I was so happy because I had my Christmas tree already up and it was the nicest tree I've ever had. The tree I had gotten was so wide and beautiful and the ornaments were only red, gold and white. I was so happy to have them here after all these years and incredibly proud to show them how nice my life was and how well I was doing.

We ate and everybody was talking about everything, from how the trip was to what they wanted to do while they were here. I needed to figure out how to best plan the week. I wanted us to do what Pauli, Jay, Tim and Nick been looking forward to do on the trip. Los Angeles is a city that never sleeps. When we were done eating, Pauli started to unpack one suitcase and I think everything in there was to me. It was Christmas light, three Lucia porcelain dolls, coffee and candy. Black licorice candy that I love and they don't have here in the US. My nieces had sent some presents for me as well and they had drawn pictures for me. That first evening, Pauli, Jay and Tim fell asleep around 10 o'clock while Nick and I were supposed to watch a movie when he said,

"Aunty, can you please tickle my back with your long nails the way you used to do when I was a kid?"

"Sure, of course Nick, come here." He sat in front of me on the couch and I gently tickle him with my nails up and down his back.

"I am so happy to see you again. It was weird, one day you were there with us and the next, you had disappeared. It was almost like you had never existed, and now when I am here with you again, it is like we were never apart," Nick said looking at me.

"I never meant to hurt or worry any of you, but I had to leave. Jared is your uncle and you boys adored him. I didn't want to take that away from you, as long as he did not harm you. I am so sorry for the confusion I've caused."

Nick caressed me, "We all understand aunty and I don't blame you. I just wanted you to know how I felt. I love you."

"I love you too Nick. It's bed time honey bunny."

We spent the week touring around the city. I showed them where I work, they met most of my friends, skate stores and a lot of shopping. We enjoyed every minute but most enjoyable was our reunion. When it was time to take them to the airport a week later, it was with sorrow in my heart. I had Pauli and the boys promise me, not to wait another eight years before they come to visit me again.

That damn fear

Devin had moved some of his things over to my apartment, but he still never said out loud how he felt for me. I'm not going to tell you our relationship was easy. We both are strong minded, independent and do things "our" way. Which wasn't the same way, and we're both hard headed instead of compromising. I was extremely scared of losing my independency and to feel that I ever needed Devin or anyone in my life, but my feelings for him grew stronger. Devin never told me how he felt, and the same confusion and insecurity from my past made its presence known again. *I am not going to assume he likes me if he doesn't tell me.'* Devin acted as if he had strong feelings for me but did not express his emotions for me in words. I didn't know how to handle my emotions and I couldn't stop my feelings for Devin from growing. I couldn't take it anymore! *I need space from Devin to let my feelings cool down.'* I wanted us to talk face to face, and when I came home from the gym, I heard Devin put his key in the door only a few minutes later. I started to explain to him how much he meant to me but that I could not live with a question mark always thinking, *does he love me or not?*

"So what do you want Hannah?"

I hesitated when I answered,

> "I don't know. I want, I need to get some space from you. I love you but I have no clue what you feel for me, or *if* you even have any romantic feelings for me."

> "So you want me to move out? I'll do it right now." Devin started packing his belongings and he didn't want to listen to me at all.

> "I don't want to, but I think it's the only way for us to remain friends. How can I know how you feel Devin? I'm not a mind reader and I need to hear if you like me in a romantic way. Not just assume that you do."

Devin didn't answer just took his last things and said, "Please do not contact me again." As he stormed out from the apartment I asked,

> "Can I at least get a hug?"

"For what?" Devin responds with an attitude and I had never seen him that upset before. I heard the door close behind him and I was torn apart. *'Smart Hannah. You chased him away because of your insecurities. But maybe it was the best solution anyway.'* I was confused because sometimes it felt like I was the best thing that ever happened to Devin and that he put me on a pedestal, just to admire me, scared he would break me. Other times he was cold as ice, completely unemotionally. Those times I didn't sense that he cared at all. Just like this time. After hearing the first sentence, he came to his own conclusion, without trying to understand what I meant. My explanation was meaningless for him and he left as if walking out from our relationship wasn't a big deal and that I didn't mean anything to him. I couldn't believe it, or honestly, I didn't want to believe Devin was gone. The difference between losing Mark and losing Devin, was that Devin chose to walk out of my life, Mark didn't. I would be lying if I said it was simple.

I struggled with my broken heart, but I struggled even more with the pain of knowing it was Devin's choice. *How could I have misjudged our relationship that badly?'* I had never thought Devin would exclude me from his life completely. People couldn't even ask me how I was doing without me starting to cry. I was missing something, a piece of myself. I wasn't complete. I texted him a few times only to let him know I was thinking of him, and got no response at all. Twice I called him regarding a matter, but he did not answer his phone.

A few months later, I realized that I had to let go of Devin. Not only out of respect for him, but for myself as well. I can't make him love me if he doesn't, and I can't force him to be my friend. When I recognized what needed to be done, I sent Devin another text message. I apologized for not respecting his wishes for me not to contact him, and promised that I would from now on. Subsequently I kept my promise to Devin and as soon as thoughts of him came up in my mind, I pushed them away by reminding myself I had to let him go.

A few weeks later, around 1:00 a.m. the ringing of my gate doorbell woke me up. I did not expect anyone so I didn't answer it, but I was curious so I looked out the window. I saw a car I recognized only too well but thought I saw wrong. *'It can't be.....'* I went out on the balcony where I could see better and exactly at that moment I realized it was who I thought it was, Devin saw me too and called my name.

My cell phone rang and Devin asked if he could come up so we could talk. I was nervous and wondered why Devin was here, but at the same time, relieved I would see him again. I put on my robe before I went to open the door. Now when I saw Devin standing in the door, I realized I had been successful to get him out of my mind but not out of my heart. For the first time I was honest to myself regarding my own emotions. I didn't try to defend and excuse myself, to myself and deny I felt the way I did about Devin. I just accepted the feeling and confessed to myself, *'I am in love with and want this man in my life.'* All I felt, despite not having seen him in a while, was happiness to see him again. Not mad, not sad or questioning Devin why he had acted the way he had. Nothing of that mattered to me and my heart was pounding like crazy. *This is how it feels to be in love. That feeling I have in my body, that extra heart beat when my phone is ringing and I hear it is his ring tone. A text message and it is from him, or when Devin walks in at 2:00 a.m. just to caress me and let me know he is home. What I feel then, is what I want to feel when I see the man I am going to spend the rest of my life with.'* A warm sensation spreads in my body and I knew for the first time in my life, I had been blessed to get a chance to experience love again. Devin was back in my life and even though he still didn't tell me in words how he felt for me, somehow I had lowered my guard and most of my insecurities disappeared.

A bump in the road

It was the Monday before Christmas and I was excited as always when it is the holiday season. I came home from work, parked my car, and grabbed our mail on the way up to the apartment. First thing I did when I entered the apartment was to turn on the lights on the tree, light some candles and unpacked my bags before I sat down to relax while I was looking through the mail. I had a letter from DMV and thought, *what can this be?* I'd already paid my registration and did not expect anything else from them. I didn't waste any time and opened the envelope right away. **"Renewal of your driver license"** and usually it's not a big deal, but somehow I got a strange feeling in my gut. I read the piece of paper and where it said "what to bring" and there it was.

That sentence I feared, and that would change my life. "Bring your SSN". I already had a feeling that I wouldn't be able to get around it this time. Devin came home for a little while, and I told him about the letter but Devin responded,

"Come on honey, you were able to work it out all the other times before, right?" He gave me one of his beautiful smiles.

"Yes you're right, but this time I don't know babe. I have a bad feeling about this."

Devin had to leave again and I put the thought of the letter aside. *'I want to go to bed with peace of mind. I'll worry about this tomorrow instead.'* Tuesday I went to work and, of course, the letter from DMV was in the back of my head.

That letter really bugged me and I decided to go to DMV and take care of it.

Wednesday morning I had a cup of coffee at work with Shannon before I took the white Acura in to fix the head light that didn't work. I brought it over to Breakmasters where I always fix my car and after Alex checked it, he told me to go to a shop where they deal with electrical issues. I know there is a shop down the street from my house and I drove over there. I was fortunate; the auto shop had time to do it immediately. I had lunch at Subway while they fixed the car and when everything was done, I drove to the DMV, only a few blocks away. As soon as I went in, I scanned the clerks to see which one I was hoping would call my number, which one I would try to charm.

There was a cute young African-American man and I thought, *yes there he is.* I got my waiting number and to my surprise, he called my number.

"Hey how can I help you?"

"I'm just here to renew my driver license, I said and handed him the letter I got in the mail."

"Do you have your old license with you?"

"Yes I do," I start digging in my purse to find my wallet. "Got it," I said and gave it to him. He started the process, then stopped and looked at me.

"Ma'am do you have a social security number?"

"No I don't." At this time I started to feel the angst coming over me. *'Stop girl and stay calm'* I thought to myself.

"Do you have a passport with you?"

"Nope."

"A green card or something?"

"No, not with me," I replied.

"I need something."

"Can you do it without?"

By the look the young clerk gave me, I knew he could read the consternation in on my face. He knew what was going on.

"I need something just to even process it in the computer." He told me with a soft voice and it was the truth. I know he would have helped me if he could. The tears rose in my eyes and I grabbed the letter from the counter and said,

"Well I guess I have to go home and get it. I'll come back later." When his eyes met mine, I could see that the young man was honestly sad that he couldn't do anything for me.
"Are you coming back today you think?"

"No, I need to go back to work. It has to be another day." I was frustrated when I got to the car, and when I drove out from the parking lot, the tears ran down my cheeks and I said aloud, *'Good job Hannah, you are screwed.'* I called Devin but it went to voicemail and I left him a message. I briefly explained what had happened and that I just needed to talk to someone who could calm me down. He was of course the first one I thought of. *'Hannah you need to calm down. I know there is a solution, but I need to stay calm so I can think straight and figure it out. I must talk to someone,'* and got a hold on Tony when I told him what was going on and Tony got upset as well. "I need my Swede here," he said and continued,

"Girl, don't stress yourself ok. Let me make some phone calls to figure out if there is any way to go around it. If there is anything else I can do meanwhile, let me know ok."

"Thank you so much Tony and let me know as soon as you hear anything. I truly appreciate your help."

"Love you girl."

"I love you too T." I got back to my job, but had to leave almost directly to pick Dave up from school. I tried to stay cool but it wasn't easy at all when my mind worked a 1000 miles an hour. *What am I going to do? I don't have a social security number, no green card and without a driver license, I'm so screwed in this country.'* All these "what if's" again. I felt so powerless and didn't know what to do. *'This is just so out of my hands and out of my control.'* I shook my head like I tried to make the worries go away. Tony called me and said he'd been talking to someone who said that the State of California had changed the laws at the beginning of the year. There was one thing I could try, and that was to research out-of-state driver license and see if there is another state where you don't need a social security number to have a driver license. The dilemma with that would be that I would need to be a residence in that state, but that wouldn't be too much of a problem. I could always work that out somehow. Now I just need to find a state. Dave and I just got back to the house when my phone rang and by the ringtone, I knew it was Devin.

"Hello."

"Hey honey, what's up?"

"I'm screwed man."

"What do you mean?"

"I went to the DMV and it is what I thought. I can't renew my driver license if I don't have a social security number, passport with a valid VISA, green card or something. My friend Tony spoke to a friend who said California changed the laws not too long ago but there might be a way for me to get it."

"And that is what?"

"It would be to go to another state and get a "out-of-state" license. Then, I would need an address in whatever state it would be."

"Well, check out in what state would work and we'll figure it out along the way. It will be okay. Don't worry my dear."

When I hang up with Devin, I felt a little calmer as always by talking to him, and I knew it was time to do some research for real. Of all the states I checked, it was either that you needed a social security number or something that shows I was here legally. The more time passed, is the more tense I became and could feel the panic coming closer. I told myself over and over again, *'there is a solution for everything, but you need to stay calm to think clearly.'*

A couple of days later, on Friday I called Devin when I found out there are no states as a solution to my problem; he asked me what I was going to do?

"I don't know babe, there is nothing I can do."

I was kind of mumbling and Devin heard in my voice how miserable and powerless I felt.
"Honey, listen to me. You know I'm going out of town but I want to talk to you face to face before you do anything further. Just try to take it easy this weekend and I'll see you when I get back home."

"Are you coming back before Christmas Eve?"

"Yeah I'll probably be back Monday, but I'll call you okay."

"Okay. Have fun and be safe out there sweetheart."

All this happening right before Christmas and of course this worried me. I told my closest friends. "Right now, I need all your help thinking up a solution." I took Devin's advice and knew there was nothing I could do before the holidays anyway. I will do my best to enjoy the season as much as I can. Over the weekend, I got all the shopping done. The food, gifts and I even cleaned the apartment. Everything was now ready which I was happy about. Devin called me Sunday night and said he was on his way back and would stop at home for a little while before he had to go to work. "Sure Dev, I can't wait to see you." Devin came home and I was happy to see him. I had him open one of his gifts that I had bought him and Devin opens the present with a child's excitement and smiled. That smile melts my heart every time. Devin was laughing when he opened the box, which was the old box our air mattress came in, but the box was now filled with mixed candy.

"See that's all Swedish sweets," I said and Devin replied,

"Yeah I know, but none of that is as sweet as this," he said, leaned forward and kissed me.

"Nah that's true," I giggled back to him and blushed while I pulled him even closer to me. I usually don't blush, but Devin made me feel like a teenage girl.

Devin and I tried to find out what to do about my situation and I started to feel more and more anxious but I was happy to have Devin's support and knew he would help me find the strength to go through with this. Devin truly is one of a kind. Now it was just to take day by day and do my best not to worry.

Finally found my way home

One day Devin called me and said we needed to talk. When he came home, he took my hand and sat me down on the couch next to him.

"H, I can't stand to see you this miserable. So how about we do it?"

"Dev I don't understand. What do you mean? Do what?" I said with a confused tone.

"Do you want to marry me Hannah? I am aware that we haven't talked about marriage and that we don't know where we are heading, but I know it is in the right direction, so let's give it a try H. Let's give us a try."

I was stunned for a moment. Couldn't believe what I've just heard.

"Are you serious Devin? You can't play with me like that."

He laughed aloud and stroked my hair,

"Hannah, I'm not playing."

My sky blue eyes filled with tears of happiness.

"Yes Dev. I would love to marry you."

Devin and I decided to get married in Las Vegas. Nothing big, just the two of us, him and me. That was all that mattered to me. My fairytale prince I'd been fantasizing and dreaming about all my life, had now got a face. Devin was my prince.

I had gotten a simple white dress for our wedding but the more I was thinking of it, as more I felt the urge to wear a real wedding dress, not just *a* dress. *'Hannah, this is your big day and do whatever it takes to make it perfect and make yourself happy.'* Two days before our wedding I called my friend Shannon,

"Girl, I can't get married in the dress I bought, I need a *real* wedding dress. This is happening once in my life, I know how I want it, and I'm not settling for less. I *can't* settle for less. This is going to be perfect. Can you please come with me and get a dress tomorrow?"

I heard how Shannon smiled before she answered back,

"I would love to. It will be an honor for me Hannah."

Before we hung up, we decided to talk in the morning. I went to bed but didn't get any sleep, I was too nervous thinking of my big day, only one more day and that's it. I guess I fell asleep anyway, because suddenly I am awakened by my alarm, it was time to get ready and pick out my dress. I made myself some coffee, brought it with me into the bathroom and got in the shower. When I was done drying myself, I jumped up on the sink as I always do, that way I get closer to the mirror when I put my make-up on. Just a little mascara, brush my teeth, a little lip gloss and I was ready to go. Shannon picked me up and headed down town.

I knew exactly in what area I would go to find my wedding dress, so we parked at the usual valet and started to walk up the street with all the boutiques. One boutique caught my eye with the dresses they had hanging on display, and we walked in. I saw three dresses that I know look great on me, and especially one of them caught my eye. It was a simple white dress with strings over the shoulders, hooked up in the back, which was open and with those same strings, you tightened in the back, a laced-up, corset-type back. It was the details on the dress I fell for, simple with these details and oh so elegant. I asked the girl if I could try them on. She said, "sure, just follow me" and showed us to a fitting room. I tried the two other dresses first and they both looked great, but when I put my favorite on, I knew it was the one. When I turned around and looked in the mirror, I took a deep breath and thought, *'is that really me?'*

Last time I had a reaction like that when I looked in the mirror, was at the woman shelter when I for the first time admit to myself I was an abused woman, and that woman had sorrow in her dark blue eyes. Now that same woman, 8 years later, looking in another mirror, dressed in her wedding gown and with happiness in her eyes which now switched to light blue. That shade of blue of my eyes was how I knew I was happy in my heart.

I almost started to cry, but put myself together. I looked again at the dress in the mirror. My shoulders was bare, other than the straps from the back, the dress was tight over my chest where the fabric was folded back and forth with a stripe of small light pink pearls shaped as flowers under, and beneath it start to be wider, just resting and following my body. I pulled the curtain aside and peeked out from the fitting room,

"Shannon, come here."

Shannon was out looking at the other dresses, but as soon as she turned towards me and I got eye contact with her, no words needed; I know she loved what she saw. All Shannon had to do was just to nod her head. I took the dress off again, gave it to the girl and asked if they have any tiaras as well. She showed me to a glass cabinet and showed me two of the bigger tiaras.

"I just want a small one."

"But those are just for the kids," she said.

"That's okay, I just want a small one anyway," Now suddenly I had a few other options. I knew exactly how I was going to put my hair up, Devin had told me one time before when I came from the gym, that he like when I had my hair like that. It was a great way to put it up the same way tomorrow again, only with a tiara on top of it. I paid for everything, and asked the cashier if he knew any tailor who could fix the length for me, but it needs to be done today.

"Yes sure. There is a tailor just upstairs here, and he can almost certainly do it right away." The cashier handles me my bag with a wide smile.

"Thank you sir," I said and turned towards Shannon, "Let's go girl."

The tailor place was right above the store and they were not busy at all, it will be ready within an hour, he said. I put the dress back on and when I walked out from the fitting room for him to measure how much the tailor would have to take off, everyone in the tailor place, turned their heads and looked at me. Smile spreads on their faces. Surprisingly, I didn't feel nervous at all, it felt more as if I was numbed.

While we waited for my dress to be ready, we checked around in some of the other stores and it suddenly hit me that I didn't even know which suit Devin had planned on wearing. *'I have to text him and ask,'* and wrote *hey sweetheart, what color is your suit for tomorrow?* But I did not have time to wait for an answer from him. We found a pair of golden shoes and a set jeweler, which included a necklace and a pair of earrings, matching the bracelet I had bought a few weeks ago. It was time to go and pick the dress up, so when we got there, I had to try the dress again to see how it fitted me.

"Hannah, try with your shoes and accessories now when you can,"

Shannon said. I put everything on and the dress was perfect, I felt just like the fairytale princess I've been dreaming about. I pulled the curtain aside to show Shannon and look myself in the big mirror. *'If Devin didn't think I was beautiful before, he defiantly will tomorrow.'* I smiled at her.

"Wow, you really are gorgeous Hannah."

'Why was I not nervous, I am getting married tomorrow.' After I had paid for the tailoring of the dress, we were done and Shannon asked if I was hungry?

"No girl, I can't eat."

Shannon did not accept that answer and we went to a Mexican restaurant, one of our favorite places. I had a small house salad and was sipping on my Margarita when I got Devin's respond, "LOL *black, yellow tie babe"* Awesome, it will look great with my outfit. After dinner, it was time to head it over to Kathy's nail place. Kathy is the woman who does my nails and it was time to pamper our self with a pedicure and manicure. When I was there, Devin called me,

"Hey what are you up too?"

191

"Just getting my nails done." I couldn't help it, but I had a big smile on my face. Shannon and Kathy looked first at me and then at each other and was cracking up.

"What time are we leaving tomorrow H?"

"Whenever you want Dev. We have booked the chapel for 2.30 pm, so whenever you want to leave, I will be ready."

"Let us leave around 6-7 am. That way, we don't have to rush and can chill for a minute when we get there."

"Sounds good. Are you coming home tonight or picking me up in the morning?"

"I will be home tonight."

"Okay so I will see you later?" I said with a silken soft voice. I could hear Devin was laughing when he answered,

"Yeah you will see me later."

I closed my eyes for a second when we hang up and I felt the love just rush out from my heart. Devin is unique and genuine. When I looked at him, were around him or just talked to him, heard his voice, it filled me with a calming feeling, I had never before experience. "I can't wait until tomorrow," I said out loud while I opened my eyes. Kathy gave me a hug and wished me good luck but I answered her,

"Thank you. We already have the most important ingredients, a great love."

When Shannon was dropping me off at our house, I asked if she want to come up and keep me company for a little bit, now I was too jumpy to be alone. We had a glass of wine and I tried on my wedding gown again, with shoes and everything.
When I came out in the living room to show her, I suddenly start to feel a pain in my stomach, a feeling I knew all too well. I started

to feel anxious, that was the sign of fear and I looked at Shannon with worry in my eyes.

"What if he doesn't show up Shannon?" I said and my voice was shaky. You could hear the concern in my words. Shannon looked at me for a second before she gets up from her chair, came over to where I was and embraced me.

"Hannah, you are talking about Devin. He would never leave you hanging. You will be alright."

She took my face between her hands and with her thumb, wiped away a tear as it roll down my cheek.

"Of course he does."

I shook my head, tried to get rid of that awful old feeling of unrest. When I took the dress off again, I just put my pajamas on and sat down chitchat with her for another 20 minutes before it was time for Shannon to go. She was going to see Evan, the man she was dating. The last thing Shannon said before she left was,

"If you need me, just call me and I'll be there sweetie ok." What would I have done without her.

I brushed my teeth, washed my face and before I went to bed around midnight, I called Devin again. No answer, so I left him a voicemail saying I am just checking in to see when he will get home. In the back of my mind, I was scared to death that Devin would have changed his mind and not show up. I did my best to relax by talking to myself, saying everything will be just fine, but after all, I must have been exhausted and fell asleep after maybe an hour, even though there were still no Devin here and no respond back at all. I felt someone touching my arm and I turned around quickly, only to see Devin standing next to our bed looking down on me.

"I am so glad to see you," I said while I got up on my knees so I could put my arms around his neck in a warmhearted hug.

193

"You better get used to me getting in late babe."

Devin whispered in my ear, and I never been happier to see him. He had to work some more on the computer but tucked me back in bed, and now I felt at least a little calmer. Beep, beep, beep, the alarm went off and after turning it off, I turned around and stroked Devin on his head,

"Time to get up honey."

I made myself a cup of coffee and got in the shower, the bag was already packed and Devin dressed so as soon as I was done, we were ready to hit the road.

"Are you ready H?"

"Yeah as ready as I can be."

Devin took the bag while I locked the door. Just when we were ready to leave in the car, I said,

"Hold on, I forgot the information about the chapel on the table. Let me go and get it."

"I drop you by the door," Devin said while he started to manage the car out from the parking spot, and through that narrow spot on to the drive way.

"Be careful here, everyone hit the wall here sooner or later."

"Oh it's cool, I don't have any marks on my car so far."

I wasn't worried, I knew Devin was a great driver. Back and forth, but still it was hard to get his car out as his car was bigger than mine was. It was tight but Devin was sure he could manage the car out without backing up one more time and we both made faces as we heard the ugly sound when the wall scratched the metal of the car.

194

"That sounds nasty," Devin said and right at that moment, I felt the twinge of uneasiness in my stomach, and I thought I was going to puke.

"Go up and get the papers H. I will wait for you here okay."

As I walked up the stairs, my "old" chatterbox started again. *Is Devin going to blame me and give me a hell now because the car got scratched? What is he going to say? Is he mad at me? What if he don't want to marry me now?'* All this things crossed my mind and I start shivering as I grabbed the paper and told myself, *'Hannah stop it. This is an old feeling and Devin would never do anything to hurt you.'* I knew the reason I got so anxious was my past. At a situation like this, Jared would have been beating me up badly, tell me it is my fault because I had forgot the paper and I was the one who had moved in to an apartment with a messed up construction driveway as this one, so I would deserve to be taught a "lesson" or some other 'excuse'. I had not felt that old fear so clear, as I did now, for many years, and I wondered why it came so strong now when it supposes to be less than ever.

I have never been as happy as I am in the present, both with Devin and myself.
'Is this old fright ever going to leave me?' It has been eight years already. On my way downstairs again, my knees almost gave up under me and I just couldn't stop shaking. Devin was sitting there waiting for me in the car, and while we exited the gate, none of us said anything. It was all quiet in the car. I looked at him from the corner of my eye and still wondering what he was thinking? A few minutes after we entered the freeway, I put my hand on his right knee,

"I am so sorry for what happened to your car."

Devin turns his head, looking at me as he says with a smile on his face,

"It is not your fault H. I guess I spoke too fast huh."

195

Devin said with warmth in his eyes. *'Oh my GOD, thank you for blessing me with this man,'* I thought, and a big smile fired up in my face. I looked out the window and got lost in my own mind, *'on our way to tie the knot.'* I don't think I really had realized yet what was about to happen. It was almost as I thought it was too good to be true. I guess some people had given up on me getting married. Ms Independent, that was me, and I had almost given up on myself too, thinking *'I will never get married, I am way too independent and won't saddle for nothing less than the best.'* Now I was about to get the fairytale I had always dreamed of. It was hard to melt, to realize my dream was about to come true.

"H, I have some idea's written down to a project I'm working on back there, and I want you to read it and give me some feedback."

Devin woke me up from my daydreaming and I said,

"Yeah I would love to read it." I reached back to grab it from his bag. The idea's was great and while I read, I was full of pride over him. When I was done reading, I put the papers back, and Devin asked me,

"So what do you think?"

"I believe it's great and I know that you will turn the idea into an even greater reality. I want you to know one thing Devin, and that is that I am behind and beside you all the way. If there is anything I can do to help you, to make anything easier or just be around in any way, I am here twenty-four seven for you."

"Thank you babe. I really appreciate it."

The first thing we did when we got to Las Vegas, was to stop by at the Marriage Bureau to get a Marriage license and as soon as we were done there, we went to The Rio to eat their buffet. It was the best in the whole USA regarding to Devin, but I had never tried it and now I wasn't hungry at all. It felt as if my nerves was outside of my body, for heaven's sake, I was about to get married. The waitress showed us to our table,

"Now enjoy and today we have free champagne included. Would the two of you like some?"

We both said no thanks as we sat down across from each other. We took our plates and there was so much food but there was no chance that I would be able to eat. I just put a few bacon strips and sausages on my plate together with some fruit, before I returned and sat down by our table. When the server passed me, I caught her attention,

"I changed my mind; can I please have a glass of champagne?"

"Sure, would you like straight champagne, or a Mimosa? Mimosa is half-champagne and half-orange juice."

"A Mimosa sounds great, thank you."

Devin arrived with a few different plates and it made me smile to see all the food on his plates. I just ate half of my food but finished my coffee and Mimosa. When we were done, we drove down the strip and our Wedding chapel was more towards the north end, so we parked and went in to check it out. It was small but very nice with yellow, white and gold interior. We went back to the car, sitting there talking and waiting for the time to pass.

"I am going to change in the car, but you go in and change in the motel,"
Devin said. "Call me when you are done and I meet you in there."

I gave him a loving hug, squeezed a little harder before I grabbed my bag and went in to the restaurant in the lobby where the powder room was located and I were going to get ready for my wedding. I started to put eyeliner, a little more mascara and a tiny bit of blush on my cheeks before it was time to do my hair. I grabbed a little bit of hair on each side and put it together in a petite ponytail on top of my head. Like the cherry on top, I finished up by sliding in the comb of the tiny tiara between my scalp and the rubber band, so the tiara covered up the rubber band. I changed in to the wedding gown, put the shoes and

197

jewelers on and last but not least, a little touch of lip-gloss. I was done and picked up my phone,

"I am ready Dev."

"Okay my dear I will be there," He said but called me back a second later.
"I need to make a phone call, but I'll be there in ten minutes okay."

I looked myself in the mirror and again my mind went to an "old insecure" place. *Is Devin going to leave me now or is he changing his mind? I mean, we are here but maybe he got cold feet and taking off.'* I closed my eyes, *'Stop thinking like this Hannah? Devin would never do that to you and nothing is as strong as the trust between the two of you. Let the past go Hannah, Devin would give you life, not take it. You are about to make your dream come true, and you're worthy to enjoy it.'* I know I am a great woman with a heart of gold, who deserves the best, but in the back of my mind, I still hear the voices from my past, that no one can ever love me and that this is too good to be true. All my life when I have been close to get something that I really want, something has snatched it away from me in the last moment. All that belongs to my past, and I really need to let it go but am scared to death still. My whole body now starts to tremble.

That's where my phobia is coming from and I thought, *'I can't wait here, I got to go.'* I put my white jacket on, zipped it all the way to my neck, as it was chilly outside from the wind today, took all my things, pulled the dress up from the ground and hurried out from the powder room. When I walked out through the lobby, everyone stopped and starred at me. The last thing I heard before I pushed the doors open and hurried to the car was someone saying, "wow, just like Cinderella". My hair was tickling my face as I rushed to the car. After putting the bag in the backseat, I got in the passenger seat, but just when I closed the door, Devin open his mouth saying,

"Wow. H, open your jacket."

I got out from the car again and opened the zipper so Devin could look at the dress, look at me. I haven't told Devin that I had got another dress, and now he was surprised. Not a sound from Devin but his eyes told me more than words. He was delighted with what he saw. I sat down again, turned my head towards him,

"I am scared. I can't stop shaking."

He took my hand between both his and responded,

"It is okay babe. I am scared too, but we will be okay. There is nothing we can't work out, as long as we do it together. Let us go and do this now."

When I saw him stand up outside the car, he was extremely handsome. Black tuxedo, black dress shirt, yellow tie and the same kind of yellow flowers in his suit jacket as I had in my bouquet. Devin walks fast and I tried to keep up with him. I had to speed up so I could take his hand, I did not trust that my own legs would carry me any longer. We had booked the chapel for 2.30 pm and after we were done with all the paper work, it was still an hour left. The secretary told us there is a gap now if we don't want to wait. I looked at Devin, "Sure, let us start."

First, it was picture time and we went it to the chapel. I looked around and the chapel was even more beautiful now when we were going to get married I thought. It was petite but very pretty with the white wood benches, ivory colored candles and the flower arrangements that were yellow and white. In the front was drapes hanging, white on the sides and a gold velvet drape across. I suddenly realize that, with the choice of color of our outfits, we matched the colors in the chapel. The photographer had us pose for the camera in the chapel and in the little room before you walk in to the chapel. When the photographs was done, she said,

"Just wait a minute while the minister is getting everything ready for you, and then he will take care of you."

We sat down on the bench close to each other, just talking and when I looked down on my hands, I saw my knuckles were all white. I become conscious how tense I was and held the flowers in a hard grasp, just as if everything would disappear if I relaxed. I released the grasp and stretched out my wrists, did my best to stop being so worried and loosen up. I looked at Devin in the corner of my eye, and a warm feeling filled my heart. His smile, his warm truthful brown eyes and skin color, it was perfect. In addition, underneath that beautiful surface, were a great personality and a genuine heart. I had never felt something this strong, as I did now when I looked at Devin.

The minister arrived and he asked us to step back to the doors and walk slowly towards the alter where he was, as the music started. I held Devin by his arm and as we were walking, out of the blue, I felt a wave of calmness coming over me and my breathing automatically went back to normal. By his side, I felt completely safe, a sensation I haven't felt too often before in my life. I knew here by his side, is where I belong. We said our vows, promised to love each other in sickness and in health, for better and for worse, and then our "I do's". Next the minister continued,

"I now declare you husband and wife." The minister looks at Devin with a wide smile on his face, "You may kiss your bride."

I turned towards my husband and we look in to each other's eyes. Devin took both of my hands, leaned forward and at that very moment when his lips met mine in a soft kiss, I felt nothing but love in my heart. I knew I had finally found my way home.

Important! Possible signs or symptoms of DV and CDV -behavioral, social, emotional and cognitive.

<u>School age;</u>
Behavioral = Aggression, Disobedience, Acting out (frequent)

Social = Fewer and poor quality peer relations, Starting easily and frequent

Emotional/Psychological = Emotionally withdrawn or detached, Fear/ Anxiety, Depression, Low self-esteem, Shame, PTSD

Cognitive = Self-blame, Distracted, Academic problems, Difficulty trusting, Bad dreams,

<u>Adolescents:</u>
Behavioral = Dating Violence, Running away, Use of drugs or alcohol, Early sexual activity

Social = Few quality relationships, Dating violence (victim or perpetrator), Starting easily and frequently

Emotional/Psychological = Emotionally withdrawn or detached, Substance abuse, PTSD, Feeling rage/ shame

Cognitive = Short attention span, Difficulty concentrating, Defensiveness, Difficulty trusting others

Edwards Brothers Malloy
Oxnard, CA USA
February 17, 2015